DON'T
BLAME
THE
SHORTS

DON'T
BLAME
THE
SHORTS

WHY SHORT SELLERS ARE ALWAYS BLAMED FOR MARKET CRASHES AND HOW HISTORY IS REPEATING ITSELF

ROBERT SLOAN

New York   Chicago   San Francisco   Lisbon   London
Madrid   Mexico City   Milan   New Delhi   San Juan
Seoul   Singapore   Sydney   Toronto

The *McGraw·Hill* Companies

1 2 3 4 5 6 7 8 9 0   DOC/DOC   0 1 0 9

ISBN 978-0-07-163686-5
MHID 0-07-163686-2

McGraw-Hill books are available at special quantity discounts to use as premiums and sales promotions, or for use in corporate training programs. To contact a representative, please visit the Contact Us pages at www.mhprofessional.com.

This book is printed on acid-free paper.

To my wonderful wife, Elizabeth, and my sister, Suzanne.
Thank you for your faith in me.

Richard S. Whitney Before the House Judiciary Committee. The Committee
Representatives La Guardia, Michener, Tucker, Condon, Celler and

WHITNEY DENOUNCES LEGISLATION AIMED AT SHORT SELLING

Practice Is Essential to Maintaining a Stock Market, He Tells House Committee.

KEPT THE EXCHANGE OPEN

Government Regulation Would Mean a Breakdown in Efficiency, He Declares.

TRADING PROVIDES CHECKS

Shorts "Smooth the Waves, but Never Affect the Tides," He Says.

SPECIAL TO THE NEW YORK TIMES.

WASHINGTON, Feb. 24. — Short
selling: is essential to the maintenance of stock exchanges, and
stock exchanges are necessary to
provide a market for investors
Richard Whitney, president of the
New York Stock Exchange, told the
House judiciary subcommittee, today.

ne of the making of the contract is
t the owner or possessor of the
curities sold."
The judiciary subcommittee, of
hich Representative Tucker of
irginia   iman, listened
tentiv
12,0
ews.
ally
uard
as
s the
ive
auth
sho
sary

position because we w
could not carry out our
matter of trust."
His summation of tl
effect of short selling in
market, under any cond
that this practice "sm
over affects

short selling wo
the activities
according to brok
ers prefer a mar
can buy or sell at

WALL ST. DISCUSSES SHORT STOCK SALES

Friends and Foes of Practice Agree a Law Against It Would Curtail Trading Sharply.

BROKERS' PROBLEMS CITED

With Business Reduced, Value of Memberships in Exchange Also Would Shrink.

Agitation in political and oth
circles against short selling in th
securities markets has directed th
attention of brokers to effects which
legislation against that practice
would have on the volume of trading on the New York Stock
Exchange and on the value of memberships in the Exchange.
The supporters and the foes of
hort selling agree that any restric-
ions on that form of trading would
esult in a sharp contraction of the
usiness done on the Exchange.
nce the value of memberships
uctuates directly with the volume
trading, a ban on short selling
uld tend to reduce that

Blow to Tradin
Barring of short
crease the problem
change firms, whose
been reduced during
years by the decrease
tivity and the decli
prices. Since their comn
with the prices of sec
decline of more than 70
the average of stock l
resulted in a large rec
these revenues. In Septem
more than f

SHORT SELLING OFTE A SUBJECT FOR DEBAT

"Bear" Operators, Censured by Pr dent Hoover, Have Stanch Defend as Well as Sharp Critics

By EUGENE M. LOKEY.

THE public reaction to President Hoover's recent censure
of "certain gentlemen" "who
been selling short in the

ably, the short selling con
Meanwhile, certain Sen
Representatives in Congre
manding legislative restr
prevent the dislocation of

CONTENTS

                1987–Present   123

                Epilogue   141

                Appendix: *New York Times* Articles   161

                • "Vote Wide Inquiry on Short Selling"
                  March 4, 1932   163
                • "Bears Planned Raid, Senators
                  Were Told"
                  April 9, 1932   166
                • "Bear Raid Inquiry Opens"
                  April 11, 1932   169
                • "List of Shorts on the Stock Exchange
                  on April 8 as Given Out by the Senate"
                  April 21, 1932   177

                Glossary   179

                Notes   191

                References   205

                Index   233

PREFACE

Well, that was what you were supposed to do.

— RESPONSE TO THE AUTHOR, AS A
TEENAGER, FROM A WALL STREET
LEGEND WHO WAS COMMENTING ON
JOE KENNEDY'S SHORT-SELLING PROFITS
MADE DURING THE 1929 CRASH

You can make money in a lot of ways and be celebrated. Corporate raiders are regularly lionized on the covers of *Fortune* and *BusinessWeek*; tech gurus are lauded for their entrepreneurship; media and movie executives are revered for their creative genius; even oil companies are often given favorable treatment. In America, you can stick two trinkets together for the first time and sell it, and someone will call it revolutionary. However, you short a company's overvalued stock and you are automatically perceived negatively, or worse, seen as unethical, undermining American capitalism.

When markets turn sour, the public complains about excess and recklessness, greed and iniquity. People feel abused and helpless, and they hope Uncle Sam will sort through the mess and figure out whom to vilify. Amid the tumult of assigning blame, short sellers are time and again deemed culpable. It is just too convenient to blame the investors who bet on falling stocks for stocks actually falling.

Even at a young age I was predisposed to blame the short seller.

My first experience with short selling occurred at 15 years old. One of the most senior men from an iconic Wall Street house who would later take the helm was my dad's dinner guest at home. Dad asked me to come in and say hello. It was right after the 1979 oil crisis, and I was looking for an intelligent comment to make about the market. Somehow Joe Kennedy, the first head of the SEC, came to mind, and I recounted how he shorted the market in '29, making over $15 million during the crash. It was not meant as a compliment.

The senior executive looked at me, paused, and without the slightest bit of emotion replied: "Well, that was what you were supposed to do."

At 15, I certainly had no training or experience in the ways of Wall Street, but almost instinctively I knew that what Kennedy had done was bad. How did that thought just appear in my head and come out as conventional wisdom? Why was a negative attitude toward short selling embedded in my young worldview? What is it about shorting that drives our political and financial institutions to distraction? How does short selling manage to bring Washington elites and corporate chieftains together in rare moments of solidarity to disparage its practice? Why does the financial press thrive on outing prominent short sellers in times of market turmoil while vilifying an investment technique that is as old as Wall Street itself?

These were the questions that encouraged me to write this book. As it turns out, the answers lie deep in the founding of this country and in the recurring tension between populism and capitalism, rural and urban America, Main Street and Wall Street.

The economic crisis that began in 2007 was caused by banks that had overvalued assets on their books—assets that they could not sell at a price they deemed to be reasonable. The difference between their tangible equity and what they could fetch for their illiquid assets comprised the crux of the credit crisis.

But when it came to the cause of their troubles, many Wall Street chief executives didn't point to their own illiquid balance sheets. Instead they relied on a familiar scapegoat: short sellers. It was the shorts, these executives claimed, who spread the rumors, innuendos, and lies that devalued—and in some cases, crippled—the stock prices of a number of the proudest names in finance, thus predicating the market's downturn.

Many of these same executives insisted that their own companies were awash in liquidity, their assets fairly valued, and their business models intact. But, as we know now, all was not blue sky. The system of payments that funded nearly all transactions, from the common to the most complex—from mom-and-pop establishments to multinational credit card companies—was about to freeze, dollar by dollar, business by business, sector by sector. Lehman Brothers, one of the most troubled firms on the Street, was teetering on the precipice of bankruptcy by September, and the American system of leveraged capitalism was about to fall under its own weight.

Of course, Lehman wasn't the first venerable Wall Street house to meet an abrupt demise. In March 2008, Bear Stearns was saved by a federally funded takeover by J. P. Morgan Chase. That rescue effort had set the stage for the potential bailout of Lehman and another troubled firm, AIG. Bailouts seemed logical, and most of Wall Street expected the government would step in to the rescue. No one knew the cost of having Lehman, a risk-taking and risk-mitigating investment firm that dominated the commercial paper markets, placed in Chapter 7 bankruptcy. But few expected that the government would take such a chance with the so-called Wal-Mart of the dollar. Lehman was a fixed income force that placed sovereign, corporate, and private debt everywhere in the world. Market regulators—prompted by appeals from the very CEOs they were meant to regulate—blamed Lehman's collapse on a third party: they blamed the shorts.

AS MARKETS PLUMMET, HISTORY REPEATS ITSELF

To be fair, short sellers have made very convenient scapegoats for nearly a century, since, by definition, they profit from the losses of others. Short sellers are the investors who borrow stock shares and sell them, and hope to profit by buying them back at a lower price. In a typical transaction, a short seller would borrow stock from a broker that had it in inventory; then he or she would sell the stock at a certain price with the hope of buying it back at a lower one. In other words, when a stock declines, the short seller benefits. Equally important, it is one investment that is ubiquitous and yet seems to fall outside of most people's grasp.

Short selling, at its very essence, is an *investment technique* used to create a profit when a stock's price falls. There are a number of reasons to short sell: a company's business model might appear fundamentally wrong, its earnings potential might seem off, or, in some cases, there may be suspicions about fraud or faulty accounting. But most shorting is done to *offset the risk* of holding a convertible bond, of betting on the spread of a merger arbitrage, or of isolating the interest rate risk in index arbitrage.

There are two steps to executing a short sale. First, the prospective short seller must look into the possibility of borrowing shares, a practice called a "locate." (Virtually every major bank has a department with the sole task of lending shares and money to clients that either want leverage or want to short stock.) Locating the shares from a bank or broker is usually executed through the prime brokerage department, which is essentially a bank for investment professionals. Most people use banks for credit lines, home mortgages, business loans, home equity, and car loans. The prime broker offers similar services for the investment professional who manages a stock or bond portfolio, and it performs these services through its prime brokerage departments.

At the outset, a short seller must get permission from a broker that the broker has shares the short seller can borrow and deliver to a buyer. In order to borrow the shares, the short seller must pledge collateral, in the form of cash, high-quality bonds, or equities, to secure the borrowing of the shares. There is an interest rate charged for borrowing these shares, and it can be very high, sometimes as much as 50 percent in interest charged per year. Once it is determined that he or she can borrow the shares, the prospective short seller sells the shares through a broker and delivers the borrowed shares to settle the transaction.

The short seller wants the price of the stock to decline. In a typical transaction, a short seller would borrow stock from a broker that had it in inventory, then he or she would sell a stock at, say, $50 a share in the hope of buying it back below $50. If the stock fell to $40, for example, and the short seller deemed that was enough of a return to justify the risk taken, he or she would buy, or "cover," the shares at $40 and book a $10 profit minus the interest rate charges to borrow the shares. The short seller would also return the borrowed shares to the broker and redeem the pledged collateral.

Despite the reputation it has received in the public forum, shorting is an essential part of our financial system. It provides the all-important liquidity the market needs, and it is the linchpin for why certain capital markets even exist. When Great Britain's departure from the gold standard further roiled the markets in 1931, the New York Stock Exchange briefly banned shorting. Market-makers had no ability to provide liquidity for transactions, and prices were soon artificially squeezed higher. Two days later, the ban was repealed.[1]

But because the short selling of a stock, by its very nature, implies a gain at another's expense, politicians have gotten a lot of mileage out of regulators blaming short sellers for market collapses, even if shorting had nothing to do with the downturn. The misguided attack on short selling, perhaps the most intricately interconnected piece of our markets, has turned into a distraction. Last fall as Lehman stood on the brink, the government did not address the vital issues of leverage ratios, lending standards, capital structure, and mark-to-market accounting rules that might have shed light on the bank's fragility. Nor did it explore the systems of using government money to purchase, loan against, and provide lines of credit on troubled assets (Troubled Asset Relief Program and Term Asset-Backed Securities Loan Facility were two such government progams) that might have propped it up. Instead, the government attacked the shorts, the amorphous, little-understood but reliable old foe who appeared more keenly aware of the banking system's own bill of health than other investors and the government itself.

At first the credit crisis and the potential insolvency of banks were blamed on the investors who were shorting stock without borrowing it first—a practice called "naked shorting." Since investors were not borrowing stock, the short seller could execute an unlimited amount of short sales. This naked shorting upsets the equilibrium of how a market absorbs shorting, potentially driving stock prices down to pennies a share.

It is puzzling why regulators tried to solve the mortgage crisis in 2008 by limiting stock borrowing in the financial sector, but nevertheless, that is what they did. In July 2008, the regulators went after shorting—the perceived enemy—by introducing new rules that curbed how sellers borrowed shares. As the stock market continued to fall, this move led to an outright ban on shorting financial shares. (As of this writing, short sellers are coming under even more federal scrutiny. After reversing itself, the Securities and Exchange Commission appears to be mulling over the possibility of imposing even more restrictive rules on short sellers once again.) Counterintuitively, a fundamental breakdown in the credit markets was being addressed by taking away liquidity in the equity markets. So instead of making the hard decision to recapitalize or fund Lehman, Washington's first move was to go after the shorts who had bet against it. In choosing to go after what it believed was the cause of Lehman's problems—rather than actually attempting to save the company—Lehman failed a few months later, launching the greatest worldwide financial collapse since the 1930s.

It was a decision that the regulators should not have made, demonstrating a distance from the marketplace and an underappreciation for the intricacy of short selling and its importance to market liquidity. Though the Fed, the SEC, and the Treasury have a few historians on their payrolls, they seem unable to use these resources effectively. The government had attempted similar moves during the 1930s—when it passed many of the regulations that revamped the markets—with virtually the same results. After the market crashed in 1929, the Senate and the House of Representatives went looking for bad guys, hunting for bear raids, short squeezes, and the investors who passed along damaging rumors about a company in order to depress its stock price. The government's attack against the shorts brought applause from the public, who wanted to find the financial villains who ruined the economy. While the attacks were politically advantageous, they dried up liquidity and the credit markets and, like today, sent the economy into a further tailspin.

The crash of 1929 is the most studied period of American financial history. How did we get the immediate reaction to the crisis so wrong and repeat many of the mistakes that were made in the aftermath of the crash? How does a country make the same mistake twice?

Because it is in our roots. The American reaction to its speculators is as fascinating as it is predictable. As far back as our founding fathers, America has always had a tenuous—and often mistrusting—relationship with speculation. From Thomas Jefferson's agrarian ideal to the populist movements to a widespread fear over the monopolistic power of barons like J. P. Morgan, the American public has often bristled with fear over the concentration of wealth and the powers allotted to those who control it. For the last three quarters of a century—and up through the writing of this book—short sellers have carried on the tainted legacy of these forebears, as a shadowy clan of self-serving investors who seek to make themselves rich at the expense of others. They're an easy target, since it is impossible to objectify their motivations: are they betting against a stock because it is overvalued or because of an ulterior motive? Despite the integral role they play in the markets, they have found themselves characterized as nefarious evildoers who not only cash in on market declines, but, in some cases, precipitate them.

The goal of this book is not to vindicate short selling as a viable practice, for anyone who knows the first thing about the stock market is already aware that short selling is an integral component of the market's very existence. Rather, the purpose of this work is to shine a light on how one common practice has become so vilified over time, and how we have become so numb to our own financial history. So much of what happened over the last year seems like a long-running play in our own financial theater. The players have changed, but the storyline and the roles played by the participants in government, regulation, speculation, banking, the press, and the public have remained remarkably stagnant despite the passage of time. History does not necessarily repeat itself in the same way, but human nature certainly does.[2]

As you will see, America's aversion to shorts is rooted in the country's very nature as a home to Main Street and Wall Street, workmen and industrialists, and yeomen and speculators. And each time that the yang outweighs the yin, politicians and an outraged public have looked for someone to blame. In fact the roots of what happened in 2008 go back even further, to a disagreement between Thomas Jefferson and Alexander Hamilton.

Robert Sloan
May 2009

Acknowledgments

My father, Stephen Samuel Sloan, wrote a book called *Thanatopfish* in which his spirit traveled through the world's waterways, seas, and rivers and pointedly exposed many of the commercial abuses and government skullduggery that stripped our waters of their bounty and precious resources. His successful attempt to take his life's experiences as a world-renowned sportsman and conservationist and tell a compelling story, one that was a forerunner to the current interest in our oceans, inspired me to write this book. I helped Dad a lot and gave him the suggestion to take his amazing deep-sea experiences and tell them to the world. I have reread *Thanatopfish* many times, and it helped me find my own voice. Even though he is no longer with us, I want to acknowledge his continuing influence on me.

Norman Mailer, who not only wrote passionately about boxing but also liked to climb in the ring himself, once was asked which was harder: writing or boxing. Mailer said: ["Writing was harder.] No doubt. I've written at times about the spooky element in writing. You go in each morning, and there's a blank page. Maybe it takes five minutes, maybe it takes an hour. Sooner or later you start writing, and then the words begin to flow. Where does that come from? You can't pinpoint it. You always wonder, 'Will it all stop tomorrow?' In that sense it's spooky. In other words, you're relying on a phenomenon that's not necessarily dependable."[1]

That fear of the whimsical nature of writing became all too real for me when I had lost my laptop—with the epilogue in it. I had not created a backup file, nor had I saved it on a memory stick. In essence, I had to start the end of the book from scratch and miss my deadline. Just as Mailer had described, I found myself relying on the inherently unreliable; capturing the original thoughts and expressions was impossible. Ten days after leaving my laptop hanging on a baggage trolley at Kennedy Airport, Liz Cummings called and said she had found my computer. This book would not have happened on time without her honesty, basic decency, and diligence in tracking me down.

This book did not come easily to me, even though many people asked where I made the time to do it. The truth is that my family sacrificed time with me so I could pursue my wild idea that I had a thesis that might actually get published. I thank my children, Stephen II and Teddy, for understanding at a very tender age that a book was important; my wife, Elizabeth, for encouraging me to pursue my ideas and believing that I could achieve them; and my sister, Suzanne, and my mom, Nancy, for their proofreading and the many good suggestions that they had.

I would like to thank all of my colleagues and partners at S3 Partners, the firm that I founded some six years ago. I could not have done this work without your support. I relied on your endless technical expertise to understand how market structure has evolved over time. A. R. Caputo, Ihor Dusaniwsky, Steve Green, Alan Howard, Mike Katz, Tony Caserta, Jeff Smith, Jeremy Slade, and Howard Sugarman all spent a lot of time relaying their thoughts, sharpening my memory, and correctly interpreting the blizzard of new rules that have come out regarding short selling. I would especially like to recognize Kate Rusie. Kate was tireless, patient, and thoughtful in helping me organize all the raw material into a book. The amount of research that went into this book was immense, and I want to thank our Stanford University graduates, Cameron Bell and Julie Klein, for all of their good ideas and thorough and detailed work.

Next I would like to thank the many friends and family members of mine and Liz's who tolerated the early exits from dinner or the absences from activities that were supposed to be shared together, but for which I had holed myself up to follow through on a new interpretation, idea, or angle. Thank you, Chris and Sandra John, John and Kim Church, Eldon and Alex Scott, Ramesh and Farida Singh, Gordon and Serena Ogden, Liz's parents, Bob and Nicki Errico, and Ken and Suzanne Bakst.

I gave an early and rough draft to many friends, who gave me ideas and suggestions to improve what I had written: Stanley Arkin, David Ballard, Alan Best, Steve Bruce, Bill Cruger, Bob Jain, J. B. L., Jeff Lewis, Geoff Menin, Doug Millett, Jim Rowen, Lisa Solbakken, Shad Stastney, and Meredith Whitney. Thank you all for taking the interest in this book and giving your honest and accurate appraisal of its content.

Thank you, James Schembari, for helping me find my own voice and for being rightly critical and forthright when the work failed to achieve what I wanted it to achieve.

I would like to thank Leah Spiro for listening to my ideas, for being my champion inside McGraw-Hill, and for putting faith in me that I would actually be able to deliver. My thanks go also to Jonathan Kelly at *Vanity Fair* for his creative instincts, insights, and intelligence.

I would like to acknowledge the ring of Wall Street executive bandits who made this book possible. Their actions and self-preservation instincts put the history of our nation in a new light for me and irritated me enough to put their actions into context.

CHAPTER 1

THE GREAT DEBATE

1790–1800

EAD OF NEW YOR...

Richard S. Whitney Before the House Judiciary Committee. The Committee...
Representatives La Guardia, Michener, Tucker, Condon, Celler and...

brought down a fresh
e upon the heads of
d professional oper-
been profiting by the
ne in wheat prices. It
of a novelty to have
oin in the rising cho-
ation, but the specu-
hood seem...

WHITNEY DENOUNCES LEGISLATION AIMED AT SHORT SELLING

Practice Is Essential to Maintaining a Stock Market, He Tells House Committee.

KEPT THE EXCHANGE OPEN

Government Regulation Would Mean a Breakdown in Efficiency, He Declares.

TRADING PROVIDES CHECKS

Shorts "Smooth the Waves, but Never Affect the Tides," He Says.

SPECIAL TO THE NEW YORK TIMES.

WASHINGTON, Feb. 24. — Short selling: is essential to the maintenance of stock exchanges, and stock exchanges are necessary to provide a market for investors, Richard Whitney, president of the New York Stock Exchange, told a House judiciary subcommittee, to day.

e of the making of the contract is
t the owner or possessor of the
urities sold."
The judiciary subcommittee, of
ich Representative Tucker of
rginia ... airman, listened
tenti...
12,0...
ews.
lly
uar...
as o...
the
ve
ath
nov...
ar...

position because we w
could not carry out our
matter of trust."
His summation of th
effect of short selling in
market, under any conc
that this practice "sm
... over affects

short selling wo
the activities
according to brok
ers prefer a mar.
can buy or sell at

Blow to Tradi...
Barring of short
crease the problem
change firms, whose
been reduced during
years by the decrease
tivity and the decli
prices. Since their comn
with the prices of sec
decline of more than 70
the average of stock
resulted in a large rec
these revenues. In Septem
more than f...

WALL ST. DISCUSSES SHORT STOCK SALES

Friends and Foes of Practice Agree a Law Against It Would Curtail Trading Sharply.

BROKERS' PROBLEMS CITED

With Business Reduced, Value of Memberships in Exchange Also Would Shrink.

Agitation in political and oth
circles against short selling in th
securities markets has directed th
attention of brokers to effects whic
legislation against that practice
would have on the volume of trad-
ng on the New York Stock
Exchange and on the value of mem-
erships in the Exchange.
The supporters and the foes of
ort selling agree that any restric-
ons on that form of trading would
sult in a sharp contraction of the
siness done on the Exchange.
ce the value of memberships
ctuates directly with the volume
rading, a ban on short selling
ld tend to...

SHORT SELLING OFTE A SUBJECT FOR DEBAT

"Bear" Operators, Censured by Pr dent Hoover, Have Stanch Defend as Well as Sharp Critics

BY EUGENE M. LOKEY.

THE public reaction to President Hoover's recent censure
of "certain gentlemen" "who

from m
over st
outrigl
of whi
Mr.
the sw
been
year
Exch
disco
shor
R
whi
said
to
wil
con
pa
la
pc

gied ou
underm
finger u
specula
erning
commo
have lo
only wi
Th...

ably, the short selling cont
Meanwhile, certain Sena
Representatives in Congre
manding legislative restri

To establish the concept of the "security of transfer," Hamilton was willing, if necessary, to reward mercenary scoundrels and penalize patriotic citizens.

—Ron Chernow

B efore we turn to the founding fathers, a few points must be made about the very nature of short selling.

Unique among financial transactions, short selling can be viewed as deeply personal, as an attack on one's own personal possessions. In 2001, when questioned about his company's unusual accounting procedures, then-Enron COO Jeffrey Skilling famously replied to a noted short seller, "Well, thank you very much, we appreciate that. . . Asshole." What's striking isn't Skilling's lack of compunction, but the fact that he had no reaction to investors who owned Enron stock and decided to sell it. In the end, of course, the short was right to suspect that Enron's books were a sham and considerably misleading.

Short selling has aroused such strong emotions that analyzing the practice dispassionately can be nearly impossible, especially since it is often misunderstood outside Wall Street. No one has any animus toward the commodities speculator who shorts wheat or oil. The person who shorts oil is a hero in this country because he wants the price to go down. But he who shorts an oil company is a villain because he wants the oil company's fortune to sour. He who shorts a corrupt energy company is only vindicated when that company's smoke-and-mirrors act has come to light. No one mentions George Soros's role in breaking the British pound by shorting the currency in 1992 as a reason to disqualify him from playing a very serious role in American politics. It is only the shorting of stocks that prompts such harsh—and strong—emotions.

The history of short sellers actually dates back to the early seventeenth century, when the very first European trade markets were born. More important, the controversy over short selling goes back just as far. The Dutch East India Company filed complaints against the Amsterdam Stock Exchange over large profits made by short sellers in 1609, which led to the first regulations on short selling the following year.[1] By the end of the seventeenth century, Amsterdam had issued a decree levying taxes on short-sale transactions. Two Dutch pamphlets on short selling from 1688, written respectively by lawyers Nicholas Muys van Holy and Joseph de la Vega, survive to this day. One, aptly titled "Confusión de Confusiones," shows how mysterious and misunderstood the practice was from its very inception.[2]

In a strange trial-and-error pattern that spanned two centuries, markets all over the West experimented with short-selling restrictions before ultimately removing them. In 1733, Sir John Barnard, a member of the British Parliament who attacked moneyed interests, introduced an act that banned naked short selling. However, the act was honored more in breach than in observance—despite heavy penalties of up to the equivalent of $500—and it was subsequently repealed in 1860.[3] In France, Napoleon's finance minister passionately lobbied the emperor on short selling's behalf but to no avail. Much like President Hoover would a century later, Napoleon couched his decision to ban the practice in patriotic terms, calling short sellers "enemies of the state."[4] Years later, however, recognizing the ban's futility, Napoleon repealed the legislation.[5] In the United States, New York prohibited short sales in 1812, only to remove the ban in 1858, when "short selling occurred with abandon."[6] In 1896 the Berlin Boerse forbade short selling, but reversed track by 1909.[7] In a strange trial-and-error pattern, markets all over the world tested short-selling restrictions and ultimately removed them.

Writing in the *New York Times*, J. Edward Meeker, the New York Stock Exchange's staff economist during the 1920s and 1930s, summarized the history of short selling with a prescience that echoes true today. "The popular misunderstanding and prejudice against short selling of securities is not new," wrote Meeker. "As long as stock exchanges of the world have existed, the short sale has been bitterly condemned, but invariably endorsed after thorough investigation or painful experience, as a vital and indispensable factor in the maintenance of free securities markets everywhere."[8]

Why had short selling been bitterly condemned, and why does it remain so today? The problem has always been, as it is now, a murky moral issue engulfing the transaction: How can a regulator possibly determine the motivation of the individual speculator? If prices fall day after day while confidence in the marketplace plummets, is it justifiable for the bear speculator to push values still lower by selling short? Is the seller motivated by righteousness or personal gain?

But these questions obscure a few important facts. First, it is the short sellers' job to hunt for fraud, inconsistency, and bad business models and to offset the risk of positions already held. Second, their profits are the proof that a company's management is not giving its shareholders an accurate picture. Third, success also requires a considerable amount of risk. Shorting is not selling those stocks that are overpriced, and getting the gearing and position weighting right. The short must endure many days, sometimes years, of being wrong before he or she is proven right. A hedge fund manager who can take a view on the markets only as long as he has use of the money—usually three months or less—must be committed and very right. The market bias and the short-term nature of his capital beg for the short to be squeezed out of his position. It runs against the human condition to accept constant daily negative feedback, the stock going up with your exposure as well, and interpret that as a positive.

The best analogy of how shorting works is in Frank Partnoy's book, *Infectious Greed*:

> Another limitation on arbitrage was the difficulty of taking a position that would increase in value when the stock went down. The basic problem was that, although it was easy to bet in favor of a particular stock, it was difficult and expensive to bet against it by shorting stock. Moreover, put options often were unavailable, too expensive, or expired too soon.[9]

Partnoy goes on to compare the stock market to a pari-mutuel betting window at a racetrack:

> It was simple to bet on a horse: you walked up to a window and bought a ticket. But how could you bet against a horse? You could try to find someone in the stands who wanted to bet on the horse, and bet with them. But that was time-consuming, and—unlike the cashier standing at the pari-mutuel window—you couldn't be assured that a random person you found would pay if she lost. Or you could do something more complicated: find someone who already had bet on the horse, borrow

their ticket, and sell that ticket so someone else, promising to pay the person if the horse won, in which case she would give you the ticket, which you then would return to the first person, along with a fee. This second plan had problems, too. Not only did it have several complex steps, but a random person betting on the horse might not be persuaded that *you* would pay if she won.[10]

Most investors short stock by borrowing the shares from their brokers and selling the borrowed shares to other investors with the promise of buying back the stock and returning it to the brokers in the future.

In the 1930s, regulators in this country made shorting more difficult to execute, which is exactly why hedge fund managers get paid so handsomely: anyone who can run the gauntlet of all the upward price bias built into how we regulate short sales is rewarded handsomely by investors. So handsomely, in fact, that it has redefined wealth as we know it. (This wealth seems to be another reason why the public distrusts short sellers.) The ability to short and to buy securities on margin (use leverage) are the main differences between a hedge fund and a mutual fund. Shorting is the main justification for the compensation models that hedge funds enjoy.

Which brings us back to Enron. Even if short sellers are correct in their positions on the value of a company, they remain a walking target on account of their own wealth and their influence on the wealth of others. Then as now, Wall Street firms that short in their proprietary trading (and profit from the liquidity and fat profit margins from executing and clearing short trades for their clients) blamed the shorts for their ills in the fall of 2008. CEOs blamed short sellers for spreading rumors about their firms and demanded their arrest. CFOs blamed short sellers for distorting their conference calls and the market valuations of assets on their balance sheets. In doing so, they adopted the populist rhetoric as old as the country itself: that shorting was un-American.

However, short selling is as American as can be. From its very beginning, the country has had an uneasy relationship with specula-tion and the compensation that comes with it. Many felt in 1790, as many do now, that compensation made through financial speculation is unjust, and short selling is the most unjust of all. When our coun-try began, there were arguments over compensation and the transfer of security rights, debates that turned out to be the forebearer for how we now feel about shorting.

HAMILTON, JEFFERSON, AND THE FIGHT OVER ASSUMPTION

In the early days of our republic the economic foundation of the coun-try was in disarray. The debt of the federal government was vast, as was that of the states, each of which had its own currency, not to mention debt and tariff laws. Some states were creditworthy, some were not, and most paid the soldiers who had helped win the Revolutionary War merely in IOUs.

In 1790, in order to steady the economy, Treasury Secretary Alexan-der Hamilton consolidated these IOUs, and other state debt, under the federal government. The move was called "assumption," and Hamilton planned to pay for it by introducing a debt scheme funded by new taxes and the use of western land as collateral. Before Hamil-ton's plan was enacted, skillful investors and speculators—some very close to Hamilton—began purchasing these depressed instruments from soldiers and other debt holders, creating the widespread appear-ance of arbitrage. The states' debt and IOUs were trading at very large discounts to par, some as low as 15 cents on the dollar.

A vast fortune might be made if investors could locate state creditors and purchase their claims at a discount. Senator Robert Morris, considered by some to be the wealthiest man in America, sent agents scurrying to the western region of his home state, Pennsylvania, to buy up cheap paper from unsuspecting citizens. Congressman James Wadsworth sent two ships to South Carolina for the same purpose. The result was that before assumption took place, or even before many people knew about Hamilton's plan, a significant number of soldiers and other holders of state debt had unloaded it at a steep discount to New York speculators. Better to receive some money, the soldiers and debt holders thought, than none at all. To the debt holders, the speculators seemed to be gambling that the federal government would step in and assume this debt.

Actually, for many of these speculators it wasn't much of a gamble. They knew the new government was about to approve assumption, and the speculators—which included political leaders—took advantage of their inside knowledge that the federal government would guarantee the repayment of that debt.

This issue about assumption set the stage for a more than 200-year ideological split over how the country's financial interests should be run. The battle determined how southern and, later, western interests would look upon their eastern brethren.

Assumption created a twofold quandary: should speculators profit from the arbitrage opportunity that the government presented to it? Or should the original soldiers be compensated for their losses? Hamilton decided that for the greater good, the speculators should be allowed to profit. The establishment of the good credit standing of the United States was more important than the vexing issue of who should profit. The government should stand behind the transferability of bonds, no matter if the purchase occurred recently, as it had with some speculators, or much earlier, as it was with many who had faith in the new government from its earliest days.

Hamilton believed in a strong executive branch. He understood that the creation of a single unit of account upon which a national currency could be established, the right to taxation, and the right to issue debt would not only unify the country but would also give the federal government the centralized power it needed to function. But that meant there would be a very hard choice—as the philosopher Thomas Hobbes argued—about how to assure that contracts would become the underpinning of a society. Contracts had to be honored, and the buyers and sellers had to accept the consequences of their actions. The protection of property rights was at the heart of any future economic structure.

Even when reports showed that many speculators were buying up cheap state debt that would become valuable under assumption, Hamilton held his nose. He maintained that the original holders got liquidity when they wanted it, and that was compensation enough, even though their military service made them more patriotic than the speculators. At stake now was a new kind of patriotism: Hamilton thought that speculators should be rewarded for showing faith in the financing structure of the new country.

> Hamilton stole the moral high ground from opponents and established the legal and moral basis for securities trading in America: the notion that securities are freely transferable and that buyers assume all rights to profits or losses in transactions. The knowledge that government could not interfere retroactively with a financial transaction was so vital ... as to outweigh any short-term expediency. To establish the concept of the "security of transfer," Hamilton was willing, if necessary, to reward mercenary scoundrels and penalize patriotic citizens.[11]

Hamilton realized that the use of federal money to solidify the central government's ability to function was an important issue in the creation of the country. He "knew that bondholders would feel a stake in preserving any government that owed them money. If the federal government, not the states, owed the money, creditors would shift their main allegiance to the central government."[12]

On the issue of assumption, Hamilton understood that if Congress approved his plan, it would give the federal government and not the states the ability to centralize taxation, unify import tariffs, and create credit for the new republic. But these centralized powers also alerted the opposition, in this case the landed interests near the Potomac. Those northern Virginia farmers had long been land rich, cash poor, and incessantly in debt to their British creditors.[13] As Jefferson said, the Virginia planter was a "species of property annexed to certain mercantile houses in London."[14]

The high interest charged by the British banks led many—including Jefferson—to make a stark choice: purchase slaves to service the debt by producing tobacco and other cash crops, or sell their land. Jefferson, like many, remained in steep debt to the British until his death in 1826.[15]

The issue of assumption was the first step in centralizing power, which many Americans, especially Jefferson, feared. Jefferson was the counterargument to Hamilton's Federalist bent. Jefferson saw the aggregation and centralization of the government as something that could lead to monarchy and betray the ideals of the Revolution. There were great paradoxes when it came to the views of both men. Jefferson was against the notion of federal government, as he feared the expansion of executive power, and at the same time was pro free trade, yet antispeculation. Hamilton saw the benefits of the Bank of England model where a good credit standing could be used to make a country more powerful.

Hamilton wanted to centralize the methods for revenue collection. He was mercantilist in trade, but was very pro financial speculation. These polemic views established how we would feel about the concentration of financial power and how financial power and government power would become intertwined in fundamental constitutional issues that would define the limits of states' rights and expand federal authority.

So as Hamilton used the Bank of England as a model to create the First Bank of the United States, his enemies did not trust a British system that they perceived worked with the monarchy at the expense of the English legislature. Many of Hamilton's enemies also owed money to England, a foreign power that had significant influence over their personal lives. As a result, when Hamilton proposed that speculators keep the gains from the IOUs and state debt, which they could redeem at a healthy profit in the new, better credit of the republic, there was a natural negative reaction to the move. So, at the formation of the nation's credit standing, Hamilton made sure that contracts were honored and that the resulting uproar did not result in a redistribution of wealth from the new owner of U.S. debt back to the original holder of the IOUs.

We can argue whether the financial tools that Hamilton employed to fund assumption were understood in the House and Senate, but his strategy undeniably had two important results: it split the financial and political capitals of the country, and—just as significantly—it split the interests of the country into banks versus borrowers.

A CAPITAL COMPROMISE: NEW YORK IS MONEY, WASHINGTON IS POLITICS

As far as dinner parties go, one hosted by Thomas Jefferson on June 20, 1790, in New York may have been the most momentous and resonant in American history. After having seen his assumption bill rejected a handful of times in Congress, Hamilton realized that in order to pass the legislation, he would need to assuage southern fears that New York was going to become a pro-British haven where politicians and bankers intermingled. He needed to appeal to fretful southerners, particularly to Jefferson. Here was the perfect opportunity. Jefferson invited Hamilton and James Madison over to discuss a compromise of sorts that would reward land holders near the Potomac: let New York be the commercial capital, while making Philadelphia the nation's temporary—and Washington the permanent—political capital.

In a grand compromise, the three men decided that commerce would be centered in New York, but laws would be passed in Philadelphia (with a commitment to move to the Potomac eventually). Now the fear of having Anglophile speculators near the seat of government—a threat to the very nature of the country's independence—could be put to rest, or so it seemed.

Hamilton held out extraordinarily high expectations for the men he believed should steward the new republic's economy—men of wealth, but altruistic enough to value the nation's financial growth over their own. All too often, however, Hamilton's friends fell far short of his expectations, abusing their proximity to him in order to leverage their own investments. As a result, many Hamiltonians became the object of manhunts or lynch mobs, and eventually found themselves in debtors' prisons (Assistant Treasury Secretary William Duer lived out his final days in one). Thus commenced the long-standing, uneasy, and often distrustful symbiotic relationship between Main Street and Wall Street that exists to this day.

Hamilton wasn't content merely with having his bank in New York. Relying on the necessary and proper clause in the Constitution, he envisaged a bank with powers that could influence and centralize the government, even if the founding fathers had not expressly consented to that power. The bank was capitalized through the sale of stock, and the shares soared. Cognizant that many speculators were more than game, Hamilton enabled investors to buy a call option. With a $25 deposit, investors were able to buy shares at par and pay off the balance over an 18-month period.[16]

In 1791, while visiting Manhattan to celebrate the capitalization of the new bank, Jefferson observed countless examples of so-called rabble lugging bags of silver and gold to the city to buy scrip. There was such fervor for the paper that bank clerks were run over when the subscription began ("scrip" and "scrippomania" were terms for "subscription"). Their value skyrocketed and only plateaued when banks refused to extend additional credit to some of the most aggressive speculators. Thus one of the century's most exuberant lexicon entries of the period, "scrippomania," was coined.

Two things about the country's reaction to speculation became apparent from this period. First, it became clear that borrowers would tolerate continued speculation as long as they had access to credit. However, once credit tightened or disappeared altogether, speculators would be blamed. It would become the bane of the farmer to sell his products in unpredictable markets controlled by bankers, whose hands had never worked the land, thereby exacerbating an already deep-seated distrust of banks and paper in all its forms. As John Adams said:

> The stock-jobbers will become the praetorian head of the Government, at once its tool and its tyrant, bribed by its largesse and overawing it by clamours and combinations.[17]

Siding with an agrarian ideal, Jefferson, Adams, and Madison believed that making money from money was useless. "An aristocracy of bank paper is as bad as the nobility of France or England," Jefferson said.[18] "Every bank in America is an enormous tax upon the people for the profit of individuals," he remarked, dismissing bankers as swindlers and thieves,[19] and the banking system itself as an "infinity of successive felonious larcenies."[20]

But to Hamilton, it wasn't larceny at all. By modeling the First Bank of the United States after the Bank of England and joining "public authority and faith with private credit," Hamilton's central bank had the ability to unite the country.[21] The new sovereign nation could not exist, he believed, unless a government could raise money, tax, take deposits, and create credit. However, two major developments did not help dispel the notion of an urban financial elite. Nor did they pacify the concerns of weary, finger-wagging agrarians.

The first was Hamilton's *Report on the Mint* in 1792. In deciding to use a ratio of gold and silver as the medium for coins in the new American currency, Hamilton was doing what he thought was best at the time—inflating a deflated economy by expanding the money supply. He then attempted to set a federal standard by fixing the value of the dollar in each state—tying its value to the number of grams of silver and gold in each coin.[22]

Hamilton's position of "bimetallism" was met with suspicion by Adams, Jefferson, and Madison, who believed that the ratio of silver to gold in each dollar would tend to shrink such that the money supply would always favor the lender. It was, to them, a very insidious secret handshake intended to benefit eastern financial interests.

The second factor reinforcing to many the presence of an urban financial elite was Hamilton's insistence that the country allow the creation of limited liability corporations. Jefferson also saw this concept as a mechanism for private gains. He hated the idea that a corporate entity could be used for the aggregation of financial power. He favored private partnerships that had unlimited liability. He wanted litigation exposure for companies whose sole design was to make money. The threat of losing everything was a governor to greed.

By the end of the eighteenth century, two very different viewpoints on speculation had been demarcated, and a battle waged between a class that lived off its land and a risk-taking class intoxicated by the paper wealth of a concentrated banking system. This latter group— championed by Hamilton—was so at odds with the country's agrarian ideals that it reinforced Jefferson's fear that New York was inhabited by nothing more than a bunch of English-sympathizing stock jobbers who dressed like, spoke like, and wished to be the English he so detested. Put another way, the notion that it was un-American to play in the financial game is nearly as old as the country itself. The battle among the founding fathers foreshadowed how economic blame would be distributed for the next 230 years.

CHAPTER 2

WALL STREET AND MAIN STREET: THE POPULIST ARGUMENT IS BORN

1830–1907

Richard S. Whitney Before the House Judiciary Committee. The Committee...
Representatives La Guardia, Michener, Tucker, Condon, Celler and ...

WHITNEY DENOUNCES LEGISLATION AIMED AT SHORT SELLING

Practice Is Essential to Maintaining a Stock Market, He Tells House Committee.

KEPT THE EXCHANGE OPEN

Government Regulation Would Mean a Breakdown in Efficiency, He Declares.

TRADING PROVIDES CHECKS

Shorts "Smooth the Waves, but Never Affect the Tides," He Says.

SPECIAL TO THE NEW YORK TIMES.

WASHINGTON, Feb. 24. — Short selling is essential to the maintenance of stock exchanges, and stock exchanges are necessary to provide a market for investors, Richard Whitney, president of the New York Stock Exchange, told the House judiciary subcommittee, to day.

... had been no short selli...

WALL ST. DISCUSSES SHORT STOCK SALES

Friends and Foes of Practice Agree a Law Against It Would Curtail Trading Sharply.

BROKERS' PROBLEMS CITED

With Business Reduced, Value of Memberships in Exchange Also Would Shrink.

Agitation in political and oth... circles against short selling in th... securities markets has directed th... attention of brokers to effects which... legislation against that practice... would have on the volume of trad... ing on the New York Stock... Exchange and on the value of mem... berships in the Exchange.

The supporters and the foes of... short selling agree that any restric... ons on that form of trading would... sult in a sharp contraction of the... siness done on the Exchange. ... nce the value of memberships... ctuates directly with the volume of... trading, a ban on short selling... ld tend to reduce that value... kers? believe.

ne of the making of the contract is... t the owner or possessor of the... curities sold."

The judiciary subcommittee, of... hich Representative Tucker of... irginia... isman, listened... ttentiv... 12,0... ews. ... ally... uard... was q... s the... ive... uth... ho... ar...

position because we w... could not carry out our... matter of trust."

His summation of th... effect of short selling in... market, under any cond... that this practice "sn... ...ver affects...

short selling wo... the activities... according to brok... ers prefer a mar... can buy or sell at...

Blow to Tradi...
Barring of short... crease the problem... change firms, whose... been reduced during... years by the decrease... tivity and the decli... prices. Since their comn... with the prices of sec... decline of more than 70... the average of stock... resulted in a large rec... these revenues. In Septem... more than f...

SHORT SELLING OFTE... A SUBJECT FOR DEBAT...

"Bear" Operators, Censured by Pr... dent Hoover, Have Stanch Defend... as Well as Sharp Critics

BY EUGENE M. LOKEY.

THE public reaction to President Hoover's recent censure of "certain gentlemen" "who have been, selling short in the...

ably, the short selling con... Meanwhile, certain Sen... Representatives in Congre... manding legislative restr... prevent the dislocation of... ked by the "bear party..."

...upon the heads of... ...d professional oper... ...been profiting by the... ...ne in wheat prices. It... ...y of a novelty to have... ...oin in the rising cho... ...ation, but the specu... ...hood seem...

finger... specul... erning... commo... have l... only w...

from... over s... outrig... of wh... Mr... the s... been... year... Exc... disc... sho...

wh... sai... to... wi... co... p... la... party...

You shall not crucify mankind upon a cross of gold.

—WILLIAM JENNINGS BRYAN

Americans fought hard for many things during the Revolution, but that didn't mean they were opposed to certain age-old European customs. One such practice that retained popularity was a palpable dislike for paying interest to lenders whose hands were scarred merely by paper cuts accrued from clipping bond coupons. The risk of the weather-dependent agrarian life, the moral conundrum of slavery, the new and bewildering commodities markets, and the perils of transporting goods by ships around the world—all this could be tolerated, even accepted. But paying interest prompted extraordinary vitriol during the nineteenth century. It was as if, many farmers believed, northern bankers had replaced the British as an interest-receiving, corpus-owning foreign power.

Conveniently, many settlers who came to America to practice their religion freely found themselves eligible for a certain economical-ecumenical loophole: European laws that forbade Christians to collect taxes from Christians. This faith-based circumnavigation of the banking system led to both a heightened hatred of taxation and a further divide between the interests of the agrarian South and commercial North. Exacerbating this conflict was the fact that a number of nineteenth-century presidents, either in or out of office, had been swindled in speculative schemes or thrown out of their homes by bankers. Andrew Jackson, for example, as a child had seen his family evicted by a banker. It was an experience, many believed, that convinced him to veto Nicholas Biddle's appeal to recharter the Second Bank of the United States and eventually pull the government funds out.

For Jeffersonian Republicans, the phrase "the pursuit of happiness" meant owning one's own property, a small shop, or a new business. But for the Hamiltonian Federalists, the same phrase implied that the country encourage the rapid acquisition of wealth.[1] Wall Street, by extension, came to be viewed in a binary fashion: either as a supplier of economic forces that created enterprise and wealth or as an enabler of political forces that sided with tyranny, corruption, and antirepublicanism. The fact that a number of extraordinary fortunes grew out of New York, then as now, only reinforced the second opinion, and it is hardly a surprise that a number of political movements, spawned from 1830 to 1896, focused their animosity on Wall Street as the oppressor of the common man, small entrepreneur, and laborer—a loose confederation of interest groups that the 2008 McCain campaign would later invoke as "Main Street." We can see now that McCain's Main Street was born, in part, by the populist movement of the middle nineteenth century.

Main Street's early distrust of Wall Street can be seen clearly in the fight between Andrew Jackson and Nicholas Biddle over the rechartering of the Second National Bank. The First and Second Banks had created great constitutional questions that highlighted the increasingly close relationship between government and banking. The banks were turning out to be a powerful enough form of capitalism to change the nature of government, and thus the control, affiliation, and consolidation of financial power had become politically charged issues.

The debate over the rechartering of the Second Bank centered on the very nature of the institution. Would it be centralized, as Biddle hoped, or would each state have a bank of its own, as Jackson advocated? Jackson won the battle—the Second Bank's charter was not renewed and ultimately failed—but his was a Pyrrhic victory. Neither he nor the populists he represented understood the great economic forces that were just beginning to form. There would soon be a need for a fully functioning banking system to fund the needs of the important industries of the nineteenth century: whaling, mining, railroads, agriculture, oil exploration, and manufacturing.

FREDERICK JACKSON TURNER: AMERICANS ARE DEFINED BY THE FRONTIER

In 1896 William Jennings Bryan delivered a historic speech that embodied the day's populist fervor. The stage could not have been grander—the Democratic National Convention in Chicago—and the message was a familiar one: the castigation of the eastern moneyed classes whose reach was now extending across the country's great plains. While ostensibly advocating bimetallism (basing the currency on silver would aid farmers in the silver-rich West), Bryan's "Cross of Gold" address used the gold standard to stoke his constituency's fear of the ever-expanding eastern commercial interests. And it worked. At 36 years of age, Bryan would become the youngest presidential nominee in the history of his party.

Bryan's assertion that "you shall not crucify mankind upon a cross of gold" was merely an extension of an intellectual argument made a few years earlier, in 1893, by Frederick Jackson Turner in his seminal essay *The Significance of the Frontier in American History*. Discrediting the argument of his mentor, Herbert Baxter Adams, who believed that all America's significant political and cultural developments owed to her English and German ancestry, Turner claimed that it was the settlement of the West, the nascent country's manifest destiny, that had forged the American character. The cycle of settlement, and the subjugation of "savagery," had given way to a new developmental order: "explorer, trapper, and trader, through maturing agricultural stages, finally reaching the complexity of city and factory."[2]

Turner feared the extinction of the frontier meant that the forces of urbanization and industrialization would be victorious over the Jeffersonian ideals of the yeoman farmer. Turner hated the idea that the "high priests of finance"[3] were the competing vision to the one that forged the American character.

The frontier, Turner argued, was the seed of democracy. It was where savagery met civilization. But now that its horizon had been met, the forces of urbanization and industrialization threatened to take hold. In short, the development of the West meant that relationships would need to be forged with the East. Miners in Colorado and California would need material or capital from New York. Perhaps "America's unique and true democracy was the product of an expanding frontier," but that land was now controlled by interests in Washington and New York.[4] Turner may have hated the notion that those same "high priests of finance" were molesting his vision of the American character, but it was too late to stop them. Wall Street had infiltrated Main Street, from the Alleghenys to the Sierra Nevadas.

So just as the Atlantic coast had been an escape from the shackles of England, America's interior had become the next ocean to cross to find identity, freedom, purpose, and fortune. But what happened when the arms of government and Wall Street could stretch across that vast land? The western frontiersmen—the nineteenth-century incarnations of Jefferson's yeoman—with their "coarseness and strength combined with acuteness and inquisitiveness . . . restless, nervous energy; that dominant individualism," found themselves pitted against Hamiltonian adversaries whom they believed existed to profit off their own ingenuity.[5]

This fear of a disappearing way of life was behind much of the populist sentiment of the 1890s. Just as some Americans now fear that globalization and the postindustrial order will put an end to our way of life, in the 1890s they feared the coming of the industrial age. Its looming presence produced incredible angst similar to what American labor recently experienced with the rise of Japan, the Asian Tigers, Brazil, Russia, India, and China. The decline of jobs being produced here, the rise of cheap foreign labor, and an open-door trade policy have sparked fears of the disappearance of our middle class that closely parallel what Americans must have felt in the 1890s about the emerging financial and industrial order.

This conflict was evidenced in the great currency debate of the age. The men and women of the frontier feared the possibility that eastern banks would enforce a gold standard that could fundamentally threaten their existence. No different than today, people then borrowed money to finance land purchases. Back then the money supply was a function of the ratio of gold and silver backing the currency. A dilution of the ratio, more silver to gold, would in effect let the borrower refinance at a lower level as the overall currency would be devalued. For these men and women, the economy centered on land and its use. The concentration of financing power would dramatically affect the industries the settlers relied on: farming, ranching, and mining.

The gold standard, Bryan exclaimed, was controlled by the men later known as the "money trusts"—it was merely another institution to stifle the frontiersman. Bryan argued to increase the ratio of silver to gold that backed each dollar in circulation. This arrangement would benefit the western farmers, miners, and ranchers, all of whom could borrow capital in expensive dollars and pay it back in inflated, cheaper currency. The stakeholder and cattleman could preserve their financial freedom, the very reason many of them headed west in the first place, if the money they borrowed for homesteads was made more affordable. Indeed, part of Bryan's populist platform was the modern-day equivalent of readjusting a home mortgage after the contract has been signed.

Bryan understood that southerners and westerners feared moneyed trusts' ability to fund westward expansion. The people who tamed the frontier, Bryan presciently understood, would not want to be tamed by either the central government or eastern bankers.

According to Turner, land was what made democracy. He "grew up believing in the traditional conservative philosophy that the key to American democracy was the dynamic competition between men and groups who had a stake in the society . . . this stake had been, for capitalist and farmer alike, the readily available and extensive supply of land. Railroads, steel plants, and wheat production were all similar in being based on control of landed resources and wealth."[6] But the disappearance of the frontier meant that the "life blood of American democracy was gone."[7]

The men whose settlement of the land counterbalanced the rise of eastern financial interests had run out of room.

The Train Approaches

By the early years of the twentieth century, a fear of money trusts had replaced fear of eastern speculators as the great threat to the frontier. The debate over the ratio of silver and gold in the currency had morphed into a fear that an omnipotent, conspiratorial moneyed cabal existed within Wall Street. The specific concern was that this shadowy organization was manipulating the flow of credit to control commercial interests in such a way that the economy was being transformed from one dominated by raw materials to one led by the manufacturing of those raw materials for commercial application.

Thomas Jefferson had long warned of the power not only of banks but also of corporations that lusted after political and financial power. By the end of the nineteenth century, his concerns appeared clairvoyant as the formation of a number of trusts—including railroad, steel, and oil—disguised the monopolistic practices of consolidation, intimidation, and price control. But because the government could not decide how to participate in the banking system at the federal level and resolve some of the concerns it had with limited liability companies, a huge vacuum was left for speculators to fill.

The whaling ship was the technological marvel of the nineteenth century. Because it was fast and able to carry vast tonnage long distances, it became the preferred vessel for oil exploration. Whale oil was in great demand before electricity, and thus whaling, a very dangerous profession, was worth the risk. However, Americans soon found that mining for what was in the ground was more profitable than mining for what was in the ocean: gold, silver, copper, and cleaner-burning oil were more profitable than oil obtained from whaling. As the middle of the country opened up, a new system of transportation was needed to distribute these resources throughout the land. In order to serve bank-financed western mining, the horse and wagon were replaced by the railroad.

Americans, who inherently distrusted the banking industry, were thoroughly disgusted by 1907. Now not only were the trains that made westward movement possible funded by the eastern speculative forces, but that movement also benefited them. The decentralized agrarian economy that Jefferson and like-minded Democratic-Republicans envisioned now appeared to have no place in the modern industrial age, where enormous amounts of capital fell into the hands of a few captains of industry. In the banking industry, there was no greater captain than John Pierpont Morgan. How Morgan came to fill that gap vacated by the government during the period would redefine banking, finance, capital markets, and credit. And it would also put political power into the very hands that populists so feared and distrusted.

CHAPTER 3

CONGRESS ATTACKS THE MONEY TRUSTS

1907–1920

Richard S. Whitney Before the House Judiciary Committee. The Committee
Representatives La Guardia, Michener, Tucker, Condon, Celler and

WHITNEY DENOUNCES LEGISLATION AIMED AT SHORT SELLING

Practice Is Essential to Maintaining a Stock Market, He Tells House Committee.

KEPT THE EXCHANGE OPEN

Government Regulation Would Mean a Breakdown in Efficiency, He Declares.

TRADING PROVIDES CHECKS

Shorts "Smooth the Waves, but Never Affect the Tides," He Says.

SPECIAL TO THE NEW YORK TIMES.

WASHINGTON, Feb. 24. — Shor
selling: is essential to the main
tenance of stock exchanges, an
stock exchanges are necessary
provide a market for investor
Richard Whitney, president of t
New York Stock Exchange, tol
House judiciary subcommittee,
day.
had been no short sel

me of the making of the contract is
ot the owner or possessor of the
ecurities sold."

The judiciary subcommittee, of
which Representative Tucker of
Virginia   irman, listened
attenti
n 12,0
iews.
ally
Guar
was d
is th
give
auth
sho
sar

position because we w
could not carry out our
matter of trust."

His summation of tl
effect of short selling in
market, under any conc
that this practice "sn
over affects

short selling wo
the activities
according to brok
ers prefer a mar.
can buy or sell at

Blow to Tradi
Barring of short
crease the problem
change firms, whose
been reduced during
years by the decrease
tivity and the decli
prices. Since their comm
with the prices of sec
decline of more than 70
the average of stock i
resulted in a large red
these revenues. In Septem
more than f

WALL ST. DISCUSSES SHORT STOCK SALES

Friends and Foes of Practice Agree a Law Against It Would Curtail Trading Sharply.

BROKERS' PROBLEMS CITED

With Business Reduced, Value of Memberships in Exchange Also Would Shrink.

Agitation in political and oth
circles against short selling in th
securities markets has directed th
attention of brokers to effects whic.
legislation against that practice
would have on the volume of trading on the New York Stock
Exchange and on the value of memberships in the Exchange.

The supporters and the foes of
short selling agree that any restric-
ions on that form of trading would
esult in a sharp contraction of the
usiness done on the Exchange.
ince the value of memberships
uctuates directly with the volume
trading, a ban on short selling
uld tend to reduce that value
kers? believe

SHORT SELLING OFTE A SUBJECT FOR DEBA

"Bear" Operators, Censured by P dent Hoover, Have Stanch Defen as Well as Sharp Critics

BY EUGENE M. LOKEY.

THE public reaction to President Hoover's recent censure
of "certain gentlemen" who
have been, selling short in the

ably, the short selling co
Meanwhile, certain Se
Representatives in Congr
manding legislative rest
prevent the dislocation c
ked by the "bear party

You could control business but no one . . . not all the money in Christendom could control credit.

—J. P. MORGAN

A national run on the banks in October 1907 dangerously froze credit and removed liquidity from the market. Public confidence in Wall Street vanished overnight. During the crisis, J. P. Morgan seized the reins of the economy from the Treasury Department and orchestrated a massive plan to avert the collapse of several large trusts and the New York Stock Exchange itself, pooling credit from large investors and injecting capital into distressed banks, all from his Madison Avenue brownstone. Indeed, Morgan and his associates saved the country from economic ruin. However, his efforts throughout the panic had the unintended consequence of skewering him in the eye of the public, which was becoming increasingly fearful that Morgan sat at the helm of a so-called money trust more powerful than the federal government.

Morgan's dominant role in the panic of 1907 seemed to confirm all populist suspicions of a sinister concentration of power on Wall Street and sounded alarms in Washington. The government, goaded by public opinion, often looks to blame someone for economic collapses. This practice began in the modern financial world with—after years of informal inquiries—the formation of a congressional committee, which was headed by Democratic representative Arsène Pujo of Louisiana.

The Pujo Committee was called to investigate the existence and power of "money trusts." The phrase, coined by Charles Lindbergh, was a product of the public fascination with copper, steel, and oil trusts.[1] In 1912, one of the issues on which Woodrow Wilson ran for president was the cleaning up of the "vast confederacies of banks, railways, express companies, insurance companies, manufacturing corporations, mining corporations, power and development companies . . . bound together by the fact that the ownership of their stock and members of their boards of directors are controlled and determined by comparatively small and closely interrelated groups of persons who . . . may control, if they please and when they will, both credit and enterprise."[2]

Congress set out to prove that banks gained representation on the corporate boards which they financed or invested in, and that these trusts controlled the "life insurance companies, savings banks, trust companies, and similar depositaries of the people's money."[3] The *New York Times* defined the Wall Street cabal as an "established and well-defined identity and community of interest between a few leaders of finance which has been created and is held together through stock holdings, interlocking directorates, and other forms of domination over banks, trust companies, railroads, public service and industrial corporations, and which has resulted in a vast and growing concentration and control of money and credit in the hands of comparatively few men."[4] Chief prosecutor Samuel Untermyer claimed the big five banks controlled over $22 billion in capital.[5] Interlocking directorates gave the heads of the great financial institutions of the day—J. P. Morgan, Bankers Trust, First National City Bank, Kuhn, Loeb & Co., and Chase National Bank—control of 134 public and private corporations in sensitive industries such as mining, railroads, steamships, and utilities, in addition to depositaries like life insurance companies, savings banks, and trusts.

Despite the vague nature of the money trust, Morgan's colossal securities firm was the primary, if unspoken, target of the assaults from Congress. The House of Morgan stood at the top of the industry; it dominated the securities business, and was able to count most of the nation's great interstate corporations among its clients. In fact, the span of Morgan's operations was so vast that lawyer Louis Brandeis wrote at the time that "practically no large enterprise can be undertaken successfully without their participation or approval."[6] To the public and the government, it was "an informal money trust . . . that advised most of the nation's great interstate corporations and monopolized the securities business, particularly the origination, underwriting, and new distribution of stocks and bonds."[7]

The notion that there are two economies in the United States—one real and the other financial—was born in this period. Banks had become so powerful that their leaders would consider them nation-states, since they financed the country's primary industries. It was a fate that neither Jefferson nor Jackson would have feared, but for the wrong reasons. By seeing the money supply, credit creation, and credit extension as political issues rather than financial ones, Jackson and Jefferson underestimated the powerful union of faith and credit when combined for a purely economic end. The men did not comprehend that the ability of a privately held bank to create credit and influence monetary policy might be more powerful and far-reaching than a national bank chartered by the government.

J. P. Morgan himself was called to testify. But what received more press attention was when William Rockefeller, the brother of John D. Rockefeller, refused to be served a subpoena. Federal marshals surrounded his homes in Tarrytown, New York, and at 689 Fifth Avenue, in Manhattan, to compel Rockefeller to testify, but he refused to accept the subpoena. A front-page article in the *New York Times* said that extra guards watched an annex that connected Rockefeller's home to one of his daughter's. Rockefeller's doctor repeatedly told the committee that Rockefeller suffered from a severe throat condition that would prevent him from testifying.[8]

Days later, news articles said Rockefeller appeared to be a "sick man." He was seen by reporters in Key West, Florida, on his way to Honduras. Rockefeller told them he did not know the committee was looking for him. He was evidently seeking a cure for his throat ailment, which was purportedly throat cancer.

Months later the committee finally interviewed him. The testimony took place in Jekyll Island, Georgia, in Rockefeller's apartment. According to newspaper reports, the apartment was elegantly laid out for the four men who conducted the interview. The spectacle undermined the committee. How does a group of senators submit to the demands of a supposedly sick witness about where and when he should testify?

Twelve minutes after William Rockefeller had appeared as a witness in the Pujo Money Trust inquiry today, his examination ended by a fit of coughing and trembling which brought a sharp warning that the ordeal must cease or the consequences might be his sudden death. Only four questions had been asked and they were answered with great difficulty in whispers. Not a word of information had been gleaned after a six months' chase.[9]

As a postscript, Rockefeller died 10 years later, not of throat cancer, but of old age.

J. P. Morgan at least answered the committee's questions, or a select scattering of them, before he lost his memory. In fact, Morgan is best remembered for his answers to Samuel Untermyer on the foundations of the banking industry:

> *Untermyer*: Is not commercial credit based primarily upon money or property?
>
> *Morgan*: No, sir. The first thing is character.
>
> *Untermyer*: Before money or property?
>
> *Morgan*: Before money or anything else. Money cannot buy it . . . a man I do not trust could not get money from me on all the bonds in Christendom.[10]

Morgan emphasized the importance of personal relationships in the banking industry and ended his testimony by saying he had never "done any short selling in his life; did not like the practice, but would not criticize it because he did not see how it could be avoided."[11]

When pressed about people, boards, and corporations he could influence, Morgan said he could not remember any of the specifics. He also didn't know about the voting trusts organized for Bankers

Trust. He said he had never heard of the International Harvester trust until he read about it in the papers.[12] He also could not remember whether his son was a director of the National City Bank or whether there were any new issues of the New York Central securities in the past five years.

From the outset, the goal of the House Committee was to produce remedial legislation to prevent further concentration of the financial sector in New York City, restore competition in the capital markets, and democratize high finance with federal regulation.[13] Yet no legislation was ever written; the goals went unmet. The Pujo Committee tried to make the country understand how credit was manipulated and controlled by a few powerful men; it sought to explain why and how bonds were issued, money was raised, and corporations were tied together by the borrowing they did through the banks. It also tried to explain how special favors were done for the friends of these companies, and how enemies were put out of business. Most significantly, it tried to pin wrongdoing, both civilly and criminally, on Morgan, and paint Wall Street as the enemy of liberty and the working man, as William Jennings Bryan had done earlier. The Pujo hearings attempted to take a century's worth of populist fears and pin them on J. P. Morgan, but it could not lay a glove on him.

To be sure, the final report did lay the groundwork for a progressive agenda that would eventually create the Federal Reserve, pass the Clayton Antitrust Act, and ratify the Sixteenth Amendment, but the actual recommendations of the Pujo Report were never put in place. Yet to see the committee as an insignificant government exercise (one might call it "going through the motions") would be grossly inaccurate, for the hearings were the most important manifestation of populist resentment toward Wall Street at the time.

The Pujo hearings also demonstrated populist America's appetite for a villain, especially during hard economic times. The very impetus for the Pujo hearings exhibits what the acclaimed historian Richard Hofstadter has called the "paranoid style in American politics." Hofstadter recognizes the American people's tendency to make sense of their history through mythologized villains. "The enemy is clearly delineated: he is the perfect model of malice, a kind of amoral superman—sinister, ubiquitous, powerful, and cruel, sensual, luxury-loving," writes Hofstadter. "He wills, indeed he manufactures, the mechanism of history, or tries to deflect the normal course of history in an evil way. He makes crises, starts runs on banks, causes depressions, manufactures disasters, and then enjoys and profits from the misery he has produced." Hofstadter's thesis suggests a brand of history that is "distinctly personal," where major historical events result not from the confluence of political, intellectual, and economic forces, but from the consequences of a "villain's" own will. It is much easier to say one man caused the panic of 1907 than to grasp the nuanced historical development that precipitated it.

Like William Jennings Bryan before him, Arsène Pujo articulated the southern and western interests at a time when they were largely forgotten or overwhelmed by northern progress. In fact, the disparity between rural and urban America was the central problem of the modern economy that had caused the panic in the first place—so severe that in 1908 President Theodore Roosevelt established the Federal Commission on Country Life to explore the issues.[14] Mass immigration, rapid technological change, the rise of industrial combinations in steel, automobiles, and commodities, and campaigns for birth control and women's suffrage were just a few of the major cultural changes taking place that disillusioned the populist masses.[15]

The farmers' situation would only get worse. After scaling for a large overseas market during the war years, American farmers were inundated with surpluses at the war's conclusion. "Cotton slumped from a wartime high of thirty-five cents per pound to sixteen cents in 1920. Corn sank from $1.50 per bushel to fifty-two cents. Wool slid from nearly sixty cents per pound to less than twenty cents."[16] As prices crashed, farmers lacked sufficient capital to pay off loans undertaken to expand production years earlier, when the country needed them most. Helpless, many joined the trek to northern urban centers, looking for higher wages and financial stability. The sweeping changes across America all seemed to align with the interests of the northern owners of capital. So, naturally, when farmers searched for a cause for their frustration, the money trusts were a good first guess.

As financial historian Vincent Carosso observes, the Pujo hearings also exhibit a fundamental characteristic of populist and capitalist relations, one that directly feeds into the paranoid style. The problem is twofold. On the one hand, the banking industry is so complex and expertise-driven that the average American is not equipped to make sense of it all. On the other, the bankers purposefully conduct their affairs in secret and "stubbornly refuse to disclose any information whatsoever about their relationships with one another or with the corporate clients they serve." Hence, even the most curious citizens have little information to digest.

Historian David Kennedy notes that "Wall Street before the 1930s was a strikingly information-starved environment. Many firms whose securities were publicly traded did not publish regular reports or if they did issue reports, the data were so arbitrarily selected and capriciously audited as to be worse than useless. It was this circumstance that had conferred such awesome power on a handful of investment bankers like J. P. Morgan, because they commanded a virtual monopoly of the information necessary to making sound financial decisions."[17]

The dual problem of an uninformed public and a clandestine business climate fueled the flames of an ever-evolving financial conspiracy that turned, after the crash of 1929, to the short sellers.

CHAPTER 4

THE MARKETS BEFORE AND AFTER 1929

...chard S. Whitney Before the House Judiciary Committee. The Committee...
Representatives La Guardia, Michener, Tucker, Condon, Celler and...

WHITNEY DENOUNCES LEGISLATION AIMED AT SHORT SELLING

Practice Is Essential to Maintaining a Stock Market, He Tells House Committee.

KEPT THE EXCHANGE OPEN

Government Regulation Would Mean a Breakdown in Efficiency, He Declares.

TRADING PROVIDES CHECKS

Shorts "Smooth the Waves, but Never Affect the Tides," He Says.

SPECIAL TO THE NEW YORK TIMES.

WASHINGTON, Feb. 24. — Short selling is essential to the maintenance of stock exchanges, and stock exchanges are necessary to provide a market for investors, Richard Whitney, president of the New York Stock Exchange, told a House judiciary subcommittee, to-day.

"Had there been no short sellin...

e of the making of the contract is ... the owner or possessor of the ...urities sold."

...he judiciary subcommittee, of ...ch Representative Tucker of ...ginia ...isman listened ...enti... ...12,0... ...ws. ...ly ...ar... s o... ...the ...ve ...th o... ...r...

position because we w... could not carry out our... matter of trust."

His summation of th... effect of short selling in ... market, under any cond... that this practice "sn... ...over affects ...

short selling wo... the activities ... according to brok... ers prefer a mar... can buy or sell at...

Blow to Tradi...

Barring of short ... crease the problem... change firms, whos... been reduced during... years by the decrease... tivity and the decli... prices. Since their comm... with the prices of sec... decline of more than 70... the average of stock ... resulted in a large red... these revenues. In Septem... more than f...

WALL ST. DISCUSSES SHORT STOCK SALES

Friends and Foes of Practice Agree a Law Against It Would Curtail Trading Sharply.

BROKERS' PROBLEMS CITED

With Business Reduced, Value of Memberships in Exchange Also Would Shrink.

Agitation in political and oth... circles against short selling in th... securities markets has directed th... attention of brokers to effects which... legislation against that practice... would have on the volume of trad... ...g on the New York Stock ...xchange and on the value of mem... ...erships in the Exchange. ...The supporters and the foes of ...ort selling agree that any restric... ...ns on that form of trading would ...ult in a sharp contraction of the ...iness done on the Exchange. ...ce the value of memberships ...tuates directly with the volume ...rading, a ban on short selling ...d tend to reduce th...

SHORT SELLING OFTE[N] A SUBJECT FOR DEBAT[E]

"Bear" Operators, Censured by Pre[si]dent Hoover, Have Stanch Defend[ers] as Well as Sharp Critics

By EUGENE M. LOKEY.

THE public reaction to President Hoover's recent censure of "certain gentlemen" who ...ve been selling short in the...

...ably, the short selling conti...

Meanwhile, certain Sena[tors]... Representatives in Congres[s]... manding legislative restri[ction]... prevent the dislocation of t...

23 Wall operated as an arm of Washington.

—Ron Chernow referencing
J. P. Morgan's New York address

The stock market crash of 1929 has been thoroughly studied. But the market environment leading up to the crash requires the same scrutiny. During the immediate postwar period, the Dow Jones dropped 47 percent between the years 1919 and 1921, when the market hit a low of 64. The 1919 high had been the result of a rise in commodity and land speculation, which in turn caused a gold boom and made speculators rich through World War I and after.[1] In "Why Today's Crisis Is More Like 1919 Than 1930," Justice Litle quotes from James Grant's *Money of the Mind*: "Like bull markets in stocks, the bull market in farmland engendered the belief that prices would rise forever. Speculators who had no interest whatever in farming bought land for the 6 percent or 8 percent annual rise that seemed a certainty throughout the early years of the century . . . "[2]

And they had very good reason to believe more money could be made in the years ahead. The price of wheat went from 62 cents a bushel at the turn of the century to 99 cents in 1909 to $1.43 in 1916 and to $2.19 in 1919. To put the final figure in context, the price of a bushel of wheat would not return to $2.19 until 1947.[3]

During the three years after World War I, the country's fortunes fell sharply. Crop prices fell by 85 percent from their postwar peak, indicating a weakness in the structure of credit that had backed the growth.[4] Seven hundred twenty-four banks shut their doors. National City Bank nearly caused a countrywide bank run when the loans it made to Cuba for sugar speculation soured. (The price of sugar jumped fivefold in 1920, but the loans were made as prices crashed.)[5] National City faced insolvency, and in a move that would presage later attempts by the government to keep bank doors open and recognize the validity of the loans, Washington—supporting the interests of Wall Street—came to the rescue. Ferdinand Pecora, the judge who oversaw the market investigation of the Senate Committee on Banking and Currency, scathingly referred to the move as "this $25 million bailing out."[6]

By 1921 the bear market that started the new decade had ended. Over the next eight years, it rose a whopping 500 percent.[7] The absolution of National City meant premonitions and warnings did not need to be heeded. The economic conditions during the 1920s favored speculation. Banks that directly bet on speculation had been bailed out, and the desire to get rich and take more risk was amplified in an environment where the United States had a trade surplus, and credit to buy land or stocks on margin was cheap.[8] Before World War I there were 250 securities dealers; by 1929 there were 6,500.[9] There was also a growth of new products, including American Depository Receipts, which enabled the trading of foreign corporations on American exchanges, and other products that packaged Latin American debt much like collateralized debt obligations. This instrument enabled investors to buy a piece of a pool of bonds ranked from "triple A" to equity. There was also the rise of pools that manipulated stocks and the introduction of mutual funds (then called investment trusts) and holding companies like Special Purpose Acquisition Companies, which raised money in anticipation of finding an opportunity to acquire or take a stake in a stock.

Short selling was also an accepted technique, and a vibrant part of the market. In a practice that would seem completely infeasible in our age, the *Wall Street Journal* published daily interest rate charges for borrowing stock, making that vital part of short selling completely transparent. In the roaring twenties, the floor of the New York Stock Exchange even had a "loan crowd," in which specialists would give loan rates for each stock. Additionally, "aside from this group," the *New York Times* explained in 1931, "there were many informal lenders in Wall Street who established lending rates by private negotiations with borrowers."[10]

In essence, the Exchange encouraged its members to borrow and lend securities among themselves by giving transparency to the interest rate that would be charged for borrowing stocks. Stocks had a published price for reference, and the borrower could know who was loaning the security and at what price. The loan crowd has morphed into today's trillion-dollar market that has no published bids and is dominated by the largest prime brokers and custody banks.

Many of the articles in the *Wall Street Journal* showed the relationship between financing and trading. Reports about how little interest was received by the borrower indicated that there was shorting activity in a certain stock. Compare this to the momentum of margin buying and you could have a real sense of whose conviction was more ardent and committed versus those who would throw in the towel as the cost of shorting rose or who could not put up more margin to hold on to their long positions.

But tolerance for short selling dried up in the wake of the Great Crash. After the Securities and Exchange Commission was created in 1934, downtick and uptick rules were introduced, first by the NYSE itself and then by Washington, to limit how short sales could be executed. This came after the NYSE had passed rules concerning the lending of securities. Shorting quickly came to be considered unpatriotic, even shameful, and the places on the floor that publicly made a market loaning securities slowly disappeared. In the mid-1930s the *Wall Street Journal* stopped publishing the rates at which market participants could short stock. Margined stock had dried up, driving down the available pool of stock for loan; short interest fell, and volume dried up. Liquidity, the lifeblood of any market, fell, and as it did, it became very expensive for investors to get in and out of the marketplace.

Chasing away the short sellers was a purely political and hollow victory. Neither politicians, regulators, nor outraged citizens searching for a villain understood that the cash that the shorts supplied to lenders was being used to keep firms funded, thus limiting stock investment trust redemptions and keeping the balance between margin buyer and short seller operating smoothly. As interest rates rose, it was probably a good source of revenue to the market makers and specialists. Attacking the shorts also helped create the next wave of market speculation offshore, away from the labels and hysteria of public sentiment, and, more important, away from the centralized government.

This move would lead to the rise of hedge funds and prime brokerages decades later. A warning made by Richard Whitney, the head of the New York Stock Exchange, would soon come true: the speculator would eventually move offshore and pay taxes elsewhere.

THE MARKET CRASHES AND SHORT SELLERS TAKE THE BLAME

The crash of 1929 presented a number of firsts for the financial system. The problems caused by the market crash were so profound that Wall Street itself could not solve them and prop up the market as it had done before. Additionally, the crisis left the not yet two-decade-old Federal Reserve—the body was formed in 1913 after the seismic panic of 1907—unsure how to interact with the fairly new Fed governor. In short, Wall Street and Washington were breaking new ground, and the country needed an explanation.

Right after the market crash, there was a great deal of communication between New York, Washington, and the press in order to stave off panic and dampen the ripple effects (particularly close was the relationship between J. P. Morgan's president, Thomas Lamont, and President Hoover). In the past the government had tried many different ways to put liquidity into the financial system. It had created national banks and even tolerated private bank consortiums like Morgan's that "specialized in deals of strategic import, requiring sensitive contacts abroad or covert government support." The government's tolerance of Morgan went so far that "23 Wall [J. P. Morgan's New York address] operated as an arm of Washington."[11]

But this crash was different. Because Wall Street had been the de facto central bank for the country during many past crises, and the Fed's role was so new, much of the blame could be conveniently lobbed at these institutions. But with trade and the stock market continuing their decline, it was not surprising that there was a search for another villain. Whereas, historically, the public's recriminations were directed toward Hamiltonian speculators or Morganesque money trusts, in the aftermath of the 1929 stock market crash, short selling became the latest excuse for explaining economic destruction. And with that, the practice descended into a controversial—and nearly conspiratorial—realm of financial transactions in which it still resides.

It was a convenient theory, since business *was* down because of the bad stock market. Indeed, Wall Street itself *had* been reporting that "bear selling" had further unsettled the market. So the public demanded that short selling be outlawed. Yet even so hostile a critic as Samuel Untermyer, the man who cross-examined J. P. Morgan during the Pujo Committee hearings, pointed out that the Exchange "has it within its power to prevent or restrict short selling" and cautioned whether such a restriction would be advisable.[12] "The Stock Exchange authorities have given public warning that the speculative sellers of stocks whose purposes were shown by deliberate circulation of disturbing rumors would be severely disciplined. But they too have declared through their president that since normal short selling is an essential part of a free market for securities,"[13] prohibition of such sales "might result in the destruction of the market,"[14] and would therefore, in any case, be "too high a price to pay for the elimination of the few who abuse this legitimate practice."[15]

President Hoover talked the matter over with the Exchange authorities, but the White House version of the interview was careful to point out that the government had no plan to interfere with policies of the Exchange.[16] But that would not prevent Hoover from publicly linking the Depression with short selling, the alleged cause of the crash. (The president blamed the Federal Reserve for low interest rates and excess reserves, which were then used to finance the buying of stocks on margin.) Hoover, for one, had already established himself as an outspoken critic of shorting, and by 1930 he began to believe that short sellers were preventing an economic rebound. Moreover, he thought of Wall Street as a Democratic conspiracy—a rigged game where short sellers were driving down stock prices.[17] Hoover even kept a list of the names of short sellers that he believed met every Sunday afternoon to plot the destruction of the market for the forthcoming week.[18] He was convinced that others planned bear raids to defeat his reelection. (There has never been any evidence to support Hoover's claim.)

By October 1930, nearly a year after the market's day of reckoning—Black Tuesday—Hoover launched what would be a steady offensive against the New York Stock Exchange. In one move, he forced Whitney to halt the loans of stock for the purpose of short selling. (Senator Smith Brookhart of Iowa had introduced legislation banning short selling as early as January of that year.) "Short-selling was—and usually is—the chief object of attack by demagogues who believed that short sales were somehow fundamentally responsible for falling stock prices, thereby forgetting that for every short seller there must necessarily be a buyer, and also that short-selling accelerates the necessary depression-adjustment in stock prices," says Murray Rothbard in *America's Great Depression*.[19]

By 1931 Hoover began to complain to senior partners of J. P. Morgan of the existence of bear raids and short selling by Wall Street. In an effort to deflect the blame from the daft Smoot-Hawley tariffs, which raised tariffs on thousands of imported goods, and the Fed's decision to raise rates in the middle of a steep market decline, Hoover blamed the shorts for the market's malfunction. "Hoover blamed the bears for everything—low public confidence, business stagnation, and falling prices."[20]

Hoover understood the constitutional nature of his attacks on shorts. He wished to see federal oversight of the NYSE and supplant New York State's authority over the Exchange. The president's accusations were the kindling. The fire would be sparked by a harrowing tale told to Congress of a bear raid and the subsequent run of one of America'a most famous entrepreneurs.

CHAPTER 5

A Lurid Tale of Blackmail, Spies, and Lies

1932

WHITNEY DENOUNCES LEGISLATION AIMED AT SHORT SELLING

Practice Is Essential to Maintaining a Stock Market, He Tells House Committee.

KEPT THE EXCHANGE OPEN

Government Regulation Would Mean a Breakdown in Efficiency, He Declares.

TRADING PROVIDES CHECKS

Shorts "Smooth the Waves, but Never Affect the Tides," He Says.

SPECIAL TO THE NEW YORK TIMES.

WASHINGTON, Feb. 24. — Short selling: is essential to the maintenance of stock exchanges, and stock exchanges are necessary to provide a market for investors, Richard Whitney, president of the New York Stock Exchange, told a House judiciary subcommittee, today.

...d... re had been no short selling

---

of the making of the contract is the owner or possessor of the rities sold."

...e judiciary subcommittee, of ch Representative Tucker of ...inia... ...irman... listened ...ntiv... 2.0... ws. ... ...ar... ...h...

position because we w could not carry out our matter of trust."

His summation of th effect of short selling in market, under any conc that this practice "sn over affects

short selling wo the activities according to brok ers prefer a mar can buy or sell at

Blow to Tradi
Barring of short crease the problem change firms, whose been reduced during years by the decrease tivity and the decli prices. Since their comn with the prices of sec decline of more than 70 the average of stock resulted in a large red these revenues. In Septem more than f...

WALL ST. DISCUSSES SHORT STOCK SALES

Friends and Foes of Practice Agree a Law Against It Would Curtail Trading Sharply.

BROKERS' PROBLEMS CITED

With Business Reduced, Value of Memberships in Exchange Also Would Shrink.

Agitation in political and oth ircles against short selling in th ecurities markets has directed th ttention of brokers to effects which gislation against that practice ould have on the volume of trad g on the New York Stock xchange and on the value of mem- ...ships in the Exchange. ...he supporters and the foes of rt selling agree that any restric- ...s on that form of trading would ...lt in a sharp contraction of the ...ness done on the Exchange. ...e the value of memberships ...uates directly with the volume ...ading, a ban on short selling ...l tend to reduce t...

SHORT SELLING OFTEN A SUBJECT FOR DEBAT

"Bear" Operators, Censured by Pre dent Hoover, Have Stanch Defende as Well as Sharp Critics

By EUGENE M. LOKEY.

THE public reaction to President Hoover's recent censure of "certain gentlemen" who ....lling short in the

ably, the short selling conti Meanwhile, certain Senat Representatives in Congress manding legislative restric prevent the dislocation of t

Certain conspirators have themselves embarked upon a
policy of "rule or ruin," and short selling has been but one
of their weapons in clubbing those who stand in their way.

—FRANK P. PARISH

In March 1931, Hoover approved a market investigation launched by the Senate Committee on Banking and Currency. The reason behind the sudden investigation was that rumors of a $1 billion bear raid fueled by foreign interests had reached Capitol Hill. The rumors rocked the markets. As the *New York Times* reported: "These reports apparently had been heard by all those concerned with the investigation, but no one would admit knowledge of their origin."[1] The hysteria of the potential bear raid reached such a heightened pitch that then-New York congressman Fiorello LaGuardia said that a number of Wall Street houses had called him and suggested that any investigating into shorting would lead to another murderous round of selling.

Hoover's hysteria over short selling and the supposed organized effort of bears to defeat him was of the many fantasies men in power concocted to explain the crash. Yet the president's conspiratory accusations gave corporate chiefs the political cover to mimic America's chief executive and blame the shorts for their own failings and fabrications. (No less intimidating a figure than J. Edgar Hoover announced that the FBI would investigate shorting stocks and the sale of wheat by the Soviet Union. It was a hedging transaction they actually got right, and deemed a communist conspiracy against the U.S. farmer.)

In a 1932 statement read before Congress, Frank Parish, the president of the Missouri-Kansas Pipeline Co., created the modern playbook for a failing chief executive and his team, one that we grew accustomed to seeing in action in late 2008—he blamed the shorts! Parish claimed that his company was ruined and said the subsequent fall of his stock was based on a supposed bear raid. If the president could finger his diminishing reelection chances on short selling, then a corporate chief could certainly blame them for decreasing the value of his stock, couldn't he?

Parish did not actually testify in person to Congress. His deposition was read into the record by Representative William Voris Gregory, a Democrat from Kentucky, who related Parish's claim that his stock crashed because he refused to bend to the economic blackmail of the Standard Oil Company of New Jersey and a rival pipeline company, H. L. Doherty and Co. His testimony was then entered into the record of the Senate Committee on Banking and Currency, which—not to be outdone by the House—had begun its own competing investigation into short selling, bear raiding, and stock exchanges. After the hearing, the headline in the *New York Times* read: "Vote Wide Inquiry on Short Selling. Senators, Without Debate, Authorize Sweeping Investigation by Banking Committee."[2]

The story that Parish told the House Judiciary subcommittee centered on a supposed "bear raid" on the Missouri-Kansas Pipeline Co. on June 16, 1930, which he said caused the stock to fall by over 50 percent. Parish may have been the first senior executive to go down that road, but his story was a lurid tale worth remembering.

In his statement, Parish said that although he bought 100,000 shares of his company's stock, the purchase was not enough to stanch the alleged bear raid. He said he was warned about the bear raid—a cabal of short sellers organized to depress the price of the stock they short—in a meeting with L. E. Fischer, vice president of the North American Light and Power Co. Fischer was accompanied to the meeting, held a few days before the raid was supposed to begin, by a Mr. McGuire, his broker. Parish said he asked Fischer to arrange a meeting with Christy Payne, vice president of the Standard Oil Company of New Jersey. A meeting was scheduled for New York, and Fischer supposedly offered to delay the bear raid for a week. When Parish arrived in New York for that meeting, he found a short-selling gun pointed at his head. Parish was testifying to some juicy statements. No one in the short-selling testimony that followed had ever testified to the existence or the inner workings of a bear raid. Parish was explaining the brazen power that a group of speculators had over the entrepreneur chasing his version of the American dream.

Upon entering the room, Payne asked, "How do you like it?"[3] Mr. Payne was referring to the fall in stock.

Parish replied, "How do I like the market of Missouri-Kansas . . . not too bad."[4] Parish liked his stock and said so. Parish was given an ultimatum. Unless he abandoned the Missouri-Kansas Pipeline Co. and had the company sell its gas reserves to Standard Oil, and all of the pipelines and pipe contracts to H. L. Doherty's Cities Service and Co., Mo-Kan's stock would be crushed on June 16. They said he would also be bankrupt and discredited, and that he and his family would be personally attacked. In his testimony, Parish said that as an inducement to accept the proposal, Fischer offered him a 15 percent interest in the stock of the Northern States Pipelines Co. at cost.

There were other offers, and Parish went into detail about how his stock's decline was disastrous to the company and to himself. In September 1930, he had to dispose of a 50 percent interest in a Missouri-Kansas subsidiary, Panhandle Eastern Pipe Line, to a subsidiary of the Columbia Gas & Electric Co., according to *Time* magazine. Parish, as reported in the *New York Times*, added that a ring of short sellers was committed to a policy of "rule or ruin and that short selling has been but one of their weapons in clubbing those who stand in the way."[5]

Payne responded by saying that he had only met Parish once in his life and had no "business dealings with him."[6]

"The charge that we sold short the shares of that company is preposterous," Payne said. "In fact, we had no relations of any character with that company and have not taken any steps to influence or interfere with development and operations," the *New York Times* reported.[7]

Missouri-Kansas sued H. L. Doherty, Standard Oil, and North American Light and Power for $75 million. The suit charged that there was a conspiracy to break Missouri-Kansas by blocking its financing plans.

"Mr. Parish had formed Frank P. Parish & Co. to sell shares in Mo-Kan and when the Mo-Kan market collapsed, Underwriter Parish was stuck with large blocks of Pipeliner Parish's shares. Since he was financing his pipeline entirely through stock sales, no more sales meant no more money," *Time* magazine reported.[8]

How did Frank Parish find himself ensnared in a public imbroglio that shone a light on the suspicious behavior of short sellers (when it should have, perhaps, illuminated his own executive behavior)?

Here's what Parish didn't tell Congress during his March 1932 hearing.

Parish was the essence of the colorful entrepreneur. He rode the rails and hoboed across the country. He started a successful machinery business in Chicago that prospered in the wake of World War I but fell apart soon afterward. He and his brother then went into business running a boat between Michigan, where they would buy peaches on the cheap, and Chicago, where they would sell them at a nice profit.

Parish then went to Kansas City in the hopes of building a pipeline, stretching from Amarillo, Texas, all the way to Indiana. In 1928 the Missouri-Kansas Pipeline Co. was born, and Parish began selling millions of dollars in stock through a brokerage firm he owned. As owner of both the company and the underwriter, Parish was able to tout the stock and use the proceeds to build the nation's second largest pipeline. The pipeline made its way out of Texas, into the territory of his rival H. L. Doherty. The stock price soared.

The pipeline, however, never made it to Indiana under Parish's control. A few years after the supposed bear raid, in 1935, Parish and his associates were accused by the Justice Department in a Chicago federal court of mail fraud and duping shareholders as the company tumbled into receivership with losses of $35 million. The government said that Parish had grossly overvalued the worth of the company. Witnesses testified about fraudulent accounting and stock manipulation.

Parish took the stand over three days in his 1935 trial. Once again, just as he had done in the House Judiciary subcommittee, he reiterated his claims of bear raids by the company's enemies, chiefly H. L. Doherty's Cities Service Co. and Standard Oil. Parish said the prime motive for the bear raid was that the company's pipeline posed a threat to the territory of his competitor, Cities Service.

Just as he had in the House, Parish said that on Saturday, June 14, 1930, he was warned that if he did not sell out, Standard and Cities would start a bear raid on Missouri-Kansas stock on the following Monday. He repeated his House testimony almost verbatim and described his meeting with Christy Payne in New York. Parish said that when he arrived at the meeting, the raid had already begun. Payne refused to see him until after the market closed. To recoup his losses, Parish reiterated, he had to sell a 50 percent interest in another pipeline company.

One of the more juicy elements of the case was that Cities Service Co. did not come to the case with clean hands. It had hired a secretary to spy on Missouri-Kansas. The secretary, Elyse Walker, was hired by Missouri-Kansas in 1930 and had an elaborate code system to alert Cities of the information Missouri-Kansas was receiving. "Mr. Parish was referred to as a 'persimmon'; Vice President S. J. Maddin was 'pineapple'; another official was 'gooseberry'; the company was 'lemons'; the Chicago Stock Exchange was 'blackberries' and the New York Stock Exchange 'dewberries,'" *Time* reported. In 1931, Frank Parish began to grow suspicious. Walker pretended to have a nervous breakdown and quit, and Cities Service subsequently paid her $1,900.[9]

The U.S. attorney presented evidence that Parish used the name and position of his brother-in-law, Francis I. Du Pont, on the board to attract investors. Du Pont testified that "his dealings with Missouri-Kansas were entirely personal, that no other member of the family and no Du Pont company was interested."[10] The prosecutor rested his case by saying, "Was that not clear proof that Frank Parish's salesmen had misrepresented the stock they sold?"[11]

Not to the jury it wasn't. The judge instructed the jurors that a verdict of guilty could be brought only if they were sure that the defendants had "consented" to the misrepresentations. The jury acquitted Parish.

Parish's case was the classic battle between executives who push or break the rules to increase the stock valuations needed to finance the next project and the short sellers who sniff out and profit from fraud. It is a battle that has continued, relatively unchanged, for almost 80 years.

Parish was acquitted because the jury evidently felt that he was a victim of a shorting raid. In the end, he had tried to blame his inability to finance the growth of his pipeline company through the sale of stock by claiming that short sellers were denying him access to capital. He paid no price for his charade. He had fought the accusations that his company was a fraudulent enterprise by accusing the shorts of engaging in fraudulent activity themselves. It was, and continues to be, the corporate chief's sturdiest line of defense: deflect his or her own failings onto the practice of shorting.

HOOVER SETS THE STAGE FOR AN ATTACK ON THE SHORTS

Part of the reason that Frank Parish was able to successfully hide his company's mistakes by blaming the shorts is because the practice was already under scrutiny. By October 1931, shorting had come under serious attack from the government. A few months earlier, in July, President Hoover had censured "bear operators" in the wheat markets and asked them to stop under the call of "national patriotism." Hoover asked them to desist from shorting during times of national economic turbulence. He asserted that hedging transactions were permissible, but purely speculative ones should be banned. Following the president's attack on speculative short selling (which George W. Bush repeated in 2008), senators and congressmen sought to pass bills that banned the practice. A series of articles from the *New York Times* gives a flavor. "Practice of Short Selling Again Attacked as Unethical. Foes Assert No Useful Purpose, While Others Say It Is Tightly Woven into the Fabric of Modern Business" was a typical headline on October 4, 1931.[12]

The article read: "When prices on the stock market are declining heavily day after day and confidence is badly shaken, is it justifiable to allow bear speculators to force values still lower by selling short? Is it 'right?'"[13]

> Is this a gambling operation and nothing more, or does it perform a useful function? The Court of Appeals of New York answered the first part of the question a number of years ago, when it ruled that both the purchase of stocks on margin and the short sale, where the seller does not possess the shares he sells, are entirely legal. "But to make such transactions legal," the court declared, "they must contemplate an actual purchase or an actual sale of stocks by the broker, or through him." An actual sale and purchase are affected in the ordinary transaction for short account. In bucketshop technique there is no such actual purchase and sale and "the transaction is a wager and therefore illegal."[14]

The court was revalidating the importance and the legal legitimacy of shorting as done by the rules at the time. Interestingly, the court foreshadowed much of the problem that modern-day derivatives are being accused of. If the purchase and sale of the stock is an ordinary transaction, that is, not a derivative, then they are perfectly permissible. If the purchase or sale were done in a way where only the profits and losses were exchanged and not the principal amount in the transaction, then the court ruled it to be "gambling."

Short selling had pretty much been tolerated in the past as a necessary part of free speculation that reduced rising prices and put a floor—through shorting's buyback mechanism—on declining prices. But following the crash, the legal backing for shorting would come under scrutiny as the government sought to rein in the forces that had mired the country in such a mammoth predicament. The government's implied powers—that fraught constitutional question pitting the Hamiltonians against the Jeffersonians—was now a relevant question when it came to shorting. This time, the control of government finances was not the issue. The question pertained to who would control Wall Street, its revenue sources, its influence, and its standing in the economy. Who would regulate shorting and the NYSE? Was it the job of the Exchange's then-regulator, New York State, or the federal government? Short selling was at the center of the argument. In order to put short selling under Washington's control, Hoover needed to place the New York Stock Exchange—which regulated the shorting that took place on Wall Street—under the government's jurisdiction. It was a Hamiltonian-inspired power grab intended to benefit Jefferson's ancestral brethren. No one has ever denied that politics and banking make strange bedfellows.

"But these functions and advantages with which the general public has little familiarity, whereas the idea of an army of powerful relentless bears assaulting security prices, at a time when the markets are in shaky condition and no support is in sight," wrote the *Times*, "is something calculated to appeal vividly to the perceptions of every one."[15] The arguments against the shorts were designed to appeal to the uninformed and easily scared masses, and history would show this particular scapegoat strategy to be so effective that it would resurface with each subsequent financial crisis through the twenty-first century.

On that same fall day in 1931, the *Times* published another article headlined: "Wall St. Discusses Short Stock Sales. Friends and Foes of Practice Agree a Law Against It Would Curtail Trading Sharply."[16] In the article, the *New York Times* described the agitation "in political and other circles against short selling . . . [the] effects of legislation against the practice would have on the volume of trading on the New York Stock Exchange."[17]

It was in this contentious environment that the head of the NYSE, Richard Whitney, became Wall Street's top public advocate for short selling. On October 17, Whitney went to Hartford, Connecticut, to address the Chamber of Commerce. His talk, it so happened, was broadcast nationwide. The *New York Times* also reported on the address, one of the first public defenses of short selling by a major business leader, under the headline: "Whitney Declares Short Sales Vital. Exchange Head Says They Enabled Market to Stand the Shock of British Gold Move."[18]

The headline actually misunderstood what Whitney had said in his broadcast. Though Whitney did say that short selling was a vital market mechanism, it was not for the purpose of "free speculation" that the headline had implied. The 1931 address was an explanation of both the functioning of the Exchange and why shorting was an integral component of the capital markets. What Whitney said in his radio address is a fascinating look into financial history.

Whitney detailed the crisis that the New York Stock Exchange was then facing, with the British having abandoned the gold standard the month before, in September—furthering the strain the U.S. markets had endured since the 1929 market crash. There was a real concern that Britain's departure from the gold standard would force the NYSE to close for only the third time in its history. (The Exchange had also closed for a few days in 1873 and for several months at the outbreak of World War I.) The Exchange understood that closing would be far worse for stock prices than staying open and letting people trade. Worse than the uncertainty over prices would be the other problematic effects of frozen bank lines, investments, and the banking system in general. The real problem, it was believed, was not how to close, but how to open. Letting people trade could swamp prices and force stocks below their minimum trading levels, effectively shutting the Exchange. So what to do?

"There was left, however, a third expedient in which in all its long history the New York Stock Exchange had never before tried, and that was a temporary suspension of short selling. This method in our opinion possessed certain features suited to the current crisis . . . by a unanimous vote of the governing committee, short selling was forthwith suspended for that day and until future notice."[19]

In his address, Whitney explained that he had realized that the only way to provide for an orderly market—the only way to keep the Exchange open—was to release what was the market's lender of last resort: the "short squeeze."

"Additional buying power in the security market was vitally needed to achieve this result. It was certain that no buying power great enough to meet the emergency was to be found except in the short interest, created by those who had previously sold short and who were committed under their contracts to repurchase," the *Times* said in its article about the address.[20]

Whitney's point was that the shorts were the lenders of last resort in the marketplace. They had to buy back stock at some point, and that very buyback mechanism was a vital emergency reserve to tap if markets could not provide liquidity themselves. He understood that tapping that reserve and banning it were two different things. Banning shorting meant that the buyback mechanism would only happen one time. Tapping the buyback, but not banning shorting, would ensure that shorts would return, albeit smarting from the losses of being forced to buy back their shares at higher prices.

Whitney discussed bear raids in his radio address. He insisted that the Exchange did not favor them and would, under the laws that governed the Exchange, ferret them out. When investigations into bear raids were conducted by the Exchange, they never panned out. Whitney stated, "Despite the many investigations of suspicious looking cases, it has been because we have found real liquidation, rather than 'bear raiding' was responsible for declining prices."[21]

But by the end of 1932, opponents of shorting had made stock borrowing very hard by pressuring stockholders into not lending their shares. If you can't borrow stock, you can't take short positions because you cannot deliver to the buyer the shares that he bought. Brokers could use customers' assets even if the customers had not margined them, but on February 18, 1932, the Exchange announced that, effective on April 1, brokers would need written authorization before lending investors' shares.

There was time for the brokers to get the proper agreements in place, but the supply of shares to borrow shrunk, and demand was the same. The interest rate for borrowing stock skyrocketed. Stock prices jumped on the hopes that the shorts would be forced to fold due to the high cost of borrowing. Two weeks later, demand and supply were at equilibrium, and stock prices fell, with only a blip of change in the short interest.

CHAPTER 6

MR. WHITNEY HEADS TO WASHINGTON

1932

...hard S. Whitney Before the House Judiciary Committee. The Committee... Representatives La Guardia, Michener, Tucker, Condon, Celler and...

WHITNEY DENOUNCES LEGISLATION AIMED AT SHORT SELLING

Practice Is Essential to Maintaining a Stock Market, He Tells House Committee.

KEPT THE EXCHANGE OPEN

Government Regulation Would Mean a Breakdown in Efficiency, He Declares.

TRADING PROVIDES CHECKS

Shorts "Smooth the Waves, but Never Affect the Tides," He Says.

SPECIAL TO THE NEW YORK TIMES.

WASHINGTON, Feb. 24. — Short selling is essential to the maintenance of stock exchanges, and stock exchanges are necessary to provide a market for investors, Richard Whitney, president of the New York Stock Exchange, told the House judiciary subcommittee, today.

...there had been no short selling

WALL ST. DISCUSSES SHORT STOCK SALES

Friends and Foes of Practice Agree a Law Against It Would Curtail Trading Sharply.

BROKERS' PROBLEMS CITED

With Business Reduced, Value of Memberships in Exchange Also Would Shrink.

Agitation in political and oth... circles against short selling in th... securities markets has directed th... ttention of brokers to effects which... legislation against that practice... would have on the volume of trad... g on the New York Stock xchange and on the value of mem... rships in the Exchange. The supporters and the foes of rt selling agree that any restric... s on that form of trading would lt in a sharp contraction of the ness done on the Exchange. e the value of memberships uates directly with the volume ading, a ban on short selling tend to reduce t...

of the making of the contract is the owner or possessor of the urities sold."

he judiciary subcommittee, of ch Representative Tucker of ginia... irman, listened nti... ws.

position because we w... could not carry out our... matter of trust."

His summation of th... effect of short selling in market, under any con... that this practice "s... never affects

short selling wo... the activities according to brok... ers prefer a mar... can buy or sell at

Blow to Tradi...
Barring of short crease the problem... change firms, whose been reduced during years by the decrease tivity and the decli prices. Since their comm with the prices of sec decline of more than 70 the average of stock resulted in a large red these revenues. In Septem more than f...

SHORT SELLING OFTEN A SUBJECT FOR DEBAT...

"Bear" Operators, Censured by Pre... dent Hoover, Have Stanch Defende... as Well as Sharp Critics

BY EUGENE M. LOKEY.

THE public reaction to President Hoover's recent censure of "certain gentlemen" "who... ably, the short selling conti... Meanwhile, certain Senat... Representatives in Congress... manding legislative restric... prevent the dislocation of t...

*You have brought this country to the greatest panic
in history.*

            —SENATOR SMITH BROOKHART,
               REPUBLICAN FROM IOWA

*We brought this country, Sir, to its standing in the world by
speculation.*

            —RICHARD WHITNEY, PRESIDENT, NEW
              YORK STOCK EXCHANGE, APRIL 1932

Hoover's call to arms, along with Frank Parish's chilling tale
of bear-raid blackmail, prompted the House investigation, and
later the Senate, to focus on shorting. And both probes pounced
on Whitney.

Shortly after his address to the Chamber of Commerce, Whitney
went to Washington to testify in front of the House Judiciary subcommittee, and the *New York Times* reported on his testimony on the
front-page with the headline: "Whitney Denounces Legislation
Aimed at Short Selling."[1]

Whitney testified because the idea of banning, legislating, and limiting short selling was gaining momentum and there were four pieces
of legislation that were being prepared by the House and later the Senate. The irony is that the Democrats, the party that had fought against

Hamilton's intrusion into states' affairs, now wanted to usurp New York State's right to regulate an institution entrusted to it. The vehicle Congress saw as the wedge to expand federal power was the hated practice of short selling.

In his 12,000-word statement to the subcommittee, Whitney defended the NYSE. He was eloquent in his defense of shorting and why it was necessary. He had to be eloquent because he was in a subcommittee stacked with Democrats who were sponsoring bills aimed at regulating the Exchange. Representative Fiorello LaGuardia wanted to ban shorting in a time of crisis. Representative Adolph Sabath, a Democrat from Illinois, authored two bills, one to forbid shorting entirely, the other to penalize the circulation of false information that was designed to hurt stock prices. Representative Edward Austin Kelly, another Democrat from Illinois, proposed a bill that would forbid the use of the mail service in margin stock transactions that did not involve actual delivery of stock.

Representative Frank Oliver, a Democrat from New York, asked whether Whitney's conversations with President Hoover over the Exchange's practices regarding stock lending had any material effect on stock prices and whether Whitney believed that prices were helped or hurt by the new written-authorization regulation. Whitney evaded the question by saying he thought he needed the president's permission to quote him directly in testimony.

"What is the effect of the recent ruling on short selling?" Whitney was asked.[2]

"I do not believe . . . it will prevent stock from being used for lending purposes," Whitney answered.[3]

"Then what abuses did you see to correct?"[4]

"We merely tried to clarify what seemed to be a confusion in the minds of a great many people," Whitney replied.[5]

"A permissive clause is contained in every contract signed between broker and customer, under which the customers' consent is required . . . we thought it was a good thing to bring pointedly in the minds of customers their rights, although they already had them."[6]

The congressmen asked a series of questions about complaints that had been made about whether clients' stock was used for loans to shorts, and Whitney answered that it had been. Did he think that shorting would be as easy now as it always had been? Whitney said that stock would be available for lending: "Yes."

Representative Francis Bernard Condon, a Democrat from Rhode Island, asked, without mentioning the president's name, whether Whitney agreed with the "prominent official" who believed that shorting was hurting the return of prosperity.

"I believe that short selling is a necessity . . . and that it has not contributed to a decline in stock prices," Whitney replied.[7]

LaGuardia then asked Whitney questions.

"It is not a fact that the short seller sells only in a declining market? . . . But he wishes to repurchase in a declining market?"

"He wishes to buy at a lower price just as a margin buyer wishes to sell at a higher level," conceded Mr. Whitney. "The short seller is not always successful. It is an old adage that short sellers never die rich."

"But since 1929," LaGuardia observed, "we haven't had any short sellers in the bread lines."[8] The congressmen went to great lengths to show that shorting hurt the market, but Whitney patiently rebutted everything they threw at him.

LaGuardia said that the combination of short sales with long sales created a market imbalance that distorted prices to the downside. Whitney replied that he thought short sales had no more effect on the downside than margin did as an upward pressure on stocks. "They almost always balance each other out."[9]

In a great moment of historical irony given where we are today, Whitney made his case to the subcommittee by using the then Florida land boom as a reason not to ban shorting:

> If short selling had been forbidden, the course of speculative move-
> ment in stocks would have been similar to what occurs when there is
> speculation in property which cannot be sold short. The most common
> and the simplest example is undoubtedly a land boom . . . it is the will-
> ingness of people who have sold short at higher levels to buy when
> prices were breaking that helped maintain the market.[10]

Whitney explained why the lender of a stock would help an investor with the exact opposite aim and execute his short strategy: money. If the loan were profitable enough, it would compensate the lender for letting the borrower short stock. The second reason why someone would lend stock is that in the back of his mind he would know that liquidity is everything and that by contributing to the buyback mechanism of the market he would be helping to preserve its stability. "By facilitating securities loans transactions they are in fact protecting the liquidity and value of their property," he said.[11]

Who should be privy to this information? Who were these short sellers? Where should their names be published? What firms did they work for? Then, Congress could shame them and declare them un-American. Representative Condon wanted it on record that Whitney was disagreeing with the president's view on shorting.

"It has been stated [by] the author of the bill that the intention is to give the broadest possible publicity in regard to short selling," Whitney said.[12]

He continued: "Obviously, the *value* [emphasis added] of this publicity will depend on how it is given to the public . . . the authors of this bill [to ban shorting] believe that this action is an innocuous one which will give information to the public. As a practical matter it is prohibitive and in actual operation will prevent short selling."[13]

Ironically predicting the events of 2008, Whitney said that banks in the Federal Reserve System should not be prohibited from lending to any member of the NYSE, as one of the proposed bills was mandating. In the aftermath of the crash, Whitney saw that the Federal Reserve's mandate would be too narrow—that if a credit crunch was to be averted, broker dealers should be able to tap the Federal Reserve's credit facilities directly. Following the Bear Stearns collapse in 2008, this is exactly what the Fed did.

Whitney lashed out against the "voluntary" requirements that some of the antishorting bills carried in the fine print, specifically that Congress would have the power to prevent banks from extending credit to NYSE members, and banks could extend credit only if the members voluntarily submitted to the regulation up for passage.

Whitney ended his testimony that day by saying:

> Since 1929, many people have been so influenced by their personal losses that they cannot dispassionately consider the facts of the case . . . in spite of the drastic deflation in the prices of securities, the New York Stock Exchange has maintained a market for securities which has allowed the holders of stocks to sell and realize cash for their property. Even if the amount realized is less, and very much

less, than it would have been if these people sold in 1929 . . . the New York Stock Exchange stayed open and maintained the liquidity of securities.[14]

Much had happened in American history between 1790 and 1932, but the ideas of redistribution of wealth, the sanctity of financial contracts, and constitutional authority were still with us. Whitney had used the Hamiltonian logic that if you got your money when you wanted it—the very definition of liquidity—then the mechanism, no matter how distasteful (assumption and coinage in Hamilton's day), had to be defended because the nation's standing was behind every transaction. That was a matter of liberty.

WHITNEY TESTIFIES AGAIN

On April 9, 1932, the New York Times printed a front-page article about the banking committee's deciding to act on bear-raid rumors. The headline read: "Wall Street Inquiry by Senate Monday; Whitney Summoned. Reports of Efforts by Foreign Interests to Depress the Dollar Also an Influence."[15] The Senate inquiry was in response to a rumored foreign plot to drive down the dollar, Parish's bear-raid tale to the House, National City's flirtation with suspending its dividend, and the recent drop in the market. And, quite possibly, it was an effort to steal attention from the House's own investigation.

In an emergency session, the Banking and Currency Committee subpoenaed Richard Whitney and asked him to name names. The committee ordered him to expose the men who were shorting stock. The assumption was, of course, that in doing so, they had committed some sort of grievous, unpatriotic sin against their country and its financial system.

The subpoena that Whitney was served asked for the following:

- A list of all corporations in whose stock there is a short account in excess of 10,000 shares
- The short interest in each corporation that had stock shorted
- A list of all stock exchange members through whom short sales were executed
- The names of clients for which stock was sold, and the number of shares in excess of 200
- The list of all people and corporations that borrowed stock to short and the amounts borrowed

"We are going to find out about the market from the bottom, top and middle," said Senator Smith Brookhart, a Republican from Iowa. "We are going to look into Mr. Whitney's machine. We are going to get the real facts, and we think he knows them."[16]

The very question put upon Whitney may have illuminated either Washington's ignorance of the practice or, worse, a political agenda. As the Depression worsened, there were rumors about America's possible departure from the gold standard, due in part to foreign investors' lack of faith in the country's credit markets. The *Times* had even reported that $11 million in gold was removed from the vaults of the Federal Reserve to be transported on the ships *Ile de France* and *Olympic* as part of a possible plot to deplete American gold reserves. Senator Frederic Walcott; a Republican from Connecticut, said that foreign manipulation of the dollar would, according to his confidential sources, "put us off the gold standard in 60 days if they wanted to."[17] The next day, April 10, the page-one headline in the *New York Times* read: "Bears Planned Raid, Senators Were Told. Group with $1,000,000,000 Reported to Have Prepared Coup for Yesterday. LaGuardia, in House, Says Brokers Threatened a Panic if Inquiry Was Started."[18]

Even among the senators themselves, the wrestling for headlines was fierce. Senator Walcott engineered the convening of the Senate hearing, while the committee chairman, Senator Peter Norbeck, a Republican from South Dakota, was out of town. The committee decided it had President Hoover's full approval to investigate: "The President is in full accord with what we have done and is absolutely back of us," the *Times* reported.[19] In other words, the senators believed they had a white paper when it came to investigating this most misunderstood form of financial transactions.

Meanwhile, Senator Carter Glass, Democrat from Virginia, who was pushing his own banking bill, said that "the stock market investigation will not interfere with *my* bill if I have the authority to prevent it—and I think I have that authority," the *Times* reported.[20] The Senate wanted everyone to know that it would go beyond what the House had covered earlier with Whitney. But the House wasn't content to sit by idly. After hearing of the investigation started by the Senate, Representative LaGuardia claimed that anonymous brokers had threatened him by claiming they would send the market further downward if the NYSE were investigated.

Ironically, and unfortunately, both the House and Senate investigations were based on the very rumors and innuendo they were supposed to be uncovering—foreign intrigue, currency manipulation, and the unknown financial powers that launched bear raids. Once the *New York*

Times began to cover the competing investigations and hearings, newspaper headlines—the currency of Washington—delayed the very bill that would soon define banks and investment banks for over the next half century. The Senate investigation came at the expense of the Glass bill, the precursor to the Glass-Steagall Act, which separated the investment-banking arms of banks—the risk takers—from the commercial-banking arms of banks—the deposit takers—until its repeal during the Clinton administration. What turned out to be the defining piece of bank legislation was given a backseat to the investigation on shorting.

Ensconced in a political crucible teeming with allegations of foreign intrigue, financial cabals, and the competitive spirit of Washington, Richard Whitney took his—somewhat familiar and proverbially *hot*—seat before the Senate committee. "Bear Raid Inquiry Opens" ran the *Times* headline. "Whitney Holds Public Is 'Trying to Give This Country Away.' Scoffs at Tales of Plot. Senators Told '120,000,000 Bulls' of 1929 Were Real Cause of Slump. Boom-Time Politics Cited. Short Selling Accounts for Only 5 Per Cent of Stock Trading, He Testifies."[21]

Senator Brookhart started the hearing by wasting little time and getting straight to the issue, according to the *Times*. There was, he alleged, a huge group of short sellers who had hoped to make a "Black Friday out of Saturday, and that you [Whitney] had the names or knew who they were, but refused to disclose that information."[22]

Whitney responded: "I had no knowledge, Senator, of any bear raid. Our investigation, made as a result of Senator Walcott looking into the operations of our specific stocks, United States Steel, American Telephone and Telegraph, Public Service of New Jersey and Consolidated Gas of New York, showed no bear raiding, but did show great liquidation for long accounts."[23]

Then Senator Robert Steiwer, Republican of Oregon, asked Whitney whether "a liquid market is advantageous, even though it is being constantly depressed?"[24]

"I think it is vital," Whitney replied. "We have some five or six billions of loans held by our banks throughout this country on collateral security listed on the New York Stock Exchange. If the New York Stock Exchange did not have a liquid market, if that market were closed, as would in my opinion happen by the prohibition of short selling, those five or six billions of collateral loans would be frozen, and the gravity of our banking situation I do not think can be overestimated."[25] Whitney was arguing that any further reduction of market liquidity, as contemplated by the Senate committee's ideas to curtail or eliminate shorting, would have had the unintended consequence of freezing secured loans made by banks to other banks. Whitney was describing the repurchase agreement (repo) market before there even was one. When banks make loans to one another so that they can fund purchases of securities, it is called "interconnectivity" in modern-day parlance.

The heated debate continued into the following day, as the Senate committee lobbed its allegations against Whitney. "You have brought this country to the greatest panic in history," Senator Brookhart admonished.

But Whitney fought back. "We brought this country, Sir, to its standing in the world by speculation . . . you think you can affect the world by changing the rules or regulations of a stock exchange or a board of trade?" he replied.[26]

"Yes," said Senator Brookhart, "we can change them by abolishing the board of trade and the stock exchange, so far as speculation is concerned."[27]

At this point Whitney verbalized what every money manager has said for the last 100 years when confronted with the threat of unwieldy government regulation. "The people of the United States," he replied, "will go to Canada and Europe to do those very things and pay their taxes there."[28]

Whitney was also bombarded by many questions regarding the mechanics of short selling and its effect. Should short selling be abolished? the senators asked. Whitney explained that without short selling, the NYSE would have closed during the gold-standard panic caused by England. "We have been unable to find fully convincing evidence that willfully false stories as to business conditions or the condition of any particular company have been circulated by short sellers for the purpose of depressing prices . . . Short selling smoothes the waves but never affects the tides," Whitney said.[29]

Unable to strike a victorious blow, the committee pressed forward with its agenda. Whitney then was asked multiple times if he knew how bear raids operated. Had he any knowledge of a bear raid? Did he know of any stock that had been or was being rigged by bears? He said that he did not. Instead, Whitney stated a number of conclusive observations about what had happened during the 1929 crash and the subsequent market decline:

- Selling by those who needed liquidity—holders who dissolved their holdings—was the number one cause of the market decline.
- Short selling, from 1929 to 1932, was only 5 percent of all Exchange transactions.
- The banning of short sales would effectively freeze the collateral for bank loans.

- "That deflation, in part, represents a state of fear in which many people are trying to give this country of ours away."[30]
- The sale of Liberty Bonds was the start of educating the investing public, and started the speculative mania culminating in the stock market crash.
- The Exchange did not foster the bull market, but feared it. Brokers, in fact, raised margins to try to depress speculation.

Whitney then explained how short interest had fallen while prices had fallen. "If there had been no short selling of securities, I am confident that the stock exchange would have been forced to close many months ago. It was the willingness of people who had sold short at higher levels to buy when prices were breaking that helped to maintain the market," he testified.[31] Whitney understood the essential role of short selling as a way to maintain circulation at a point in the cycle where nothing else is moving. Without the short sellers, the market would go stagnant.

He said that proposed laws to restrict shorting and stock borrowing would reduce the "volume and trading on the New York Stock Exchange and the value of the memberships on the Exchange."[32] And it would potentially be a "blow to trading revenue," which was desperately needed by firms reeling from lack of volume.[33]

The "problem with abolishing the short sale," asserted Whitney, "is that it is so intricately woven into the fabric of business. That wiping it out would present enormous difficulties. It has been frequently pointed out that the contractor who agreed to build a house before he has bought the materials, the tailor who takes an order for a suit of clothes without having the cloth on hand, the manufacturer who sells goods before he has produced them, all engage in selling short. The procedure is different . . . but the principle is the same in both cases."[34]

After they were through with Whitney, the committee called other witnesses, including Matthew Chauncey Brush, head of the American International Corp., and Percy Rockefeller, scion of the Rockefeller family.

Brush was one of the biggest speculators of his day. Born in Kansas, he made his way to Boston, where his trading acumen made him the director of some 50 companies by 1929. *Time* magazine reported that he had a collection of 2,000 model elephants, some as large as a car and others smaller than a ladybug.[35] But this whimsical executive hobby wasn't enough to make Brush the ideal insensitive plutocrat to skewer. Another story—in some ways a near forebear to Tyco CEO Dennis Kozlowski's birthday party in Sardinia—embodies the wretched excesses of Brush's lifestyle.

To celebrate the gold boon in Ontario, Canada, he and some of his Wall Street operators visited the Porcupine fields as guests of McIntyre Porcupine Mines president John P. Bickell and Charles McCrea, Ontario's minister of mines. At a dinner given in a curling rink, Mr. Bickell introduced a singing quartet of miners, grimy, sweat-streaked, and dressed in their working clothes: rubber coats, boots, breeches, and helmets.

When he returned to Manhattan a few weeks later, Brush recalled what fun the trip to Canada had been, especially the quartet, so he arranged to have the singers sent by a special plane to perform the next evening at a dinner for McCrea in New York. However, Brush insisted, the miners must remain dirty and wear their work clothes to earn their $1,000 fee. But the quartet cleaned themselves up anyway. They appeared at the dinner in store-bought clothes with faces bright and shining, which infuriated Brush, who refused to let them sing. The quartet was forced to send for their work clothes. Four days later, they sang for the American Institute of Mining and Metallurgical Engineers.

However, Brush was unapologetic in his testimony to the Senate committee. "It is pathetic, the basis on which average traders buy stock. They get a circular . . . telling them that XYZ is a great buy, and they all jump in. That's no exaggeration," he said. "I don't think my short positions have any more effect on the market than a rabbit. Patriotism has no more to do with it than that inkwell."[36]

Percy Rockefeller was also called to testify. Rockefeller responded with the same amnesia that had plagued his father, William, when questioned by the Pujo Committee in 1913. When asked whether he had access to inside information because of his position on boards, Percy Rockefeller claimed he did not recall.[37]

A total of 40 men testified in front of the committee in its attempt to determine how so much money was lost. Operating pools like Anaconda Copper and Radio were investigated, but the Senate did not prove any wrongdoing and brought no charges. Senators tried but failed to get witnesses to say that the specialists on the Exchange floor gave inside tips about which pool was buying or selling.

From the public's point of view, short selling was easy to understand. To them, short sellers were not mom-and-pop operators. They attacked other people's personal possessions for profit. The men called to the House and Senate were well-known market professionals who made money from the misfortune of others. That there were fraudulent enterprises with equally fraudulent management, outrageous bubbles, or just plain crazy share prices that deserved to be shorted was not in the public's consciousness.

In April, the Senate tried to shame all those who were short stocks, and on a full page the *Times* published the names, along with addresses and photos of those who were short more than 2,500 shares of a stock and what brokerage they used. Unsurprisingly, Percy Rockefeller's name was included (see Appendix).

The Senate committee pretty much reached the same conclusion. On April 25, 1932, the committee decided that there was no evidence of rumormongering, bear raids, or other devious short selling. They may have saved themselves time from their thinly veiled assault on the short had they one history buff on the committee. After the panic of 1907, New York governor Charles Evans Hughes had convened a committee to investigate the effects of "bear sales." His conclusion, however, was that the unwinding of leveraged long positions had affected the market more than shorts had. The *New York Times* had even reminded the public of the commission only a few years earlier, in 1930, in the form of an editorial:

> This is not the first occasion on which "suppression of bear sales" has been vehemently urged. After the panic of 1907, under circumstances closely resembling those which now exist, demands for such action forced Governor Hughes to appoint an impartial committee to investigate the question. This committee contained not one member of the Stock Exchange; it was made up of such eminent economists, journalists, and practical business men as Mr. Horace White, Judge Samuel H. Ordway, Mr. Edward D. Page, and Professor John B. Clark of Columbia.
>
> In its unanimous report of 1909, the committee found that the greatest evil of the stock market was "pyramiding" of speculation for the rise on the basis of previous paper profits, now used as "margin" for still larger ventures.
>
> We have been strongly urged to advise the prohibition or limitation of short sales, not only on the theory that it is wrong to agree to sell

what one does not possess, but that such sales reduce the market price of the securities involved. We do not think that it is wrong to agree to sell something that one does not now possess but expects to obtain later. Contracts and agreements to sell, and deliver in the future, property which one does not possess at the time of the contract are common in all kinds of business. The man who has "sold short" must someday buy in order to return the stock which he has borrowed to make the short sales. Short sellers endeavor to select times when prices seem high in order to sell, and times when prices seem low in order to buy, their action in both cases serving to lessen advances and diminish declines of price.[38]

It seems clear that the House and the Senate committees were really after only one thing: big headlines that satisfied the country's populist leanings. The populist movements of the nineteenth century—the Knights of Labor, the Grange movement, the antitrust movement, and the Farmer's Alliance—all saw conspiracies.[39] For at the very front of populist fervor was an inverted way of interpreting the Civil War. The war, still searing in many people's memory, was viewed by some as a fight to free blacks. The populist movement further saw working whites as having replaced the slaves and now being under the subjugation of Wall Street bankers.

But instead of posturing for headlines, the committees should have been asking for an explanation of how profits were made from a typical margined long- and short-sale transaction. An investigation into the mundane mechanics and market infrastructure—how leverage was used and abused—would have been an interesting, and informative, lesson to explain what happened in 1929 and after. But newspapers didn't touch the topic, and it never really received any serious attention from the committees.

DICK WHITNEY GOES TO JAIL

After his testimony before the Senate, Richard Whitney returned home to New York a hero. Having so eloquently defended not only short selling but also the New York Stock Exchange itself, he was named head of the NYSE for two more terms. Indeed, Whitney had confirmed that Wall Street now had in him an effective and knowledgeable advocate to counter the populist attacks from Washington. There was just one problem: Whitney was a thief.

Few could claim bluer blood than Whitney himself. His ancestors had come over on the *Arabella* in 1630. Just like FDR, he was schooled at both the prestigious Groton School, in Massachusetts, and Harvard, where he was captain of the baseball team and a member of the elitist Porcellian Club. Whitney had come to Wall Street as a young man and bought a seat on the Exchange at 23, using his brother's contacts to make Richard Whitney and Co. the principal brokerage agent for J. P. Morgan. He joined the very exclusive New York Yacht Club—where Morgan was one of the club's first commodores—along with the Links, the Racquet, and the Knickerbocker Club. He married the daughter of the president of the Union League Club, and his brother was married to the daughter of a Morgan partner.

Whitney was no ordinary broker. He executed a large majority of J. P. Morgan's trades, and in 1929, during the initial market crash, he famously strode across the Exchange floor to make a $205 bid for U.S. Steel when the stock was trading at below $200. J. P. Morgan, in its customary role as financier to the market, was trying to buoy the market with that bid and chose Whitney to deliver this message. With Morgan's backing, Whitney was made the head of the Exchange the following year and ended up serving four terms.

Whitney also wanted to be a player and decided that the end of Prohibition would make him rich, so he and a partner bought a company called Distilled Liquor. Its main product was Jersey Lightning, which required aging to be potable and was popular during Prohibition. Whitney eventually bought a significant stake in the stock. The stock did poorly, so Whitney continued to pledge stock he bought in open market as collateral for more cash to reinvest in Distilled Liquor stock. Margin calls began, but he had no liquidity.

Whitney had actually been bankrupt in 1932, the same year he testified before the Senate (J. P. Morgan loaned him $474,000 to try and stave off his creditors), but he continued to try to buy more stock. In 1938, as a result of new rules, the Exchange decided to have all members report their capital positions on a more frequent and transparent basis. The jig was up; Whitney had no money, and it was plain for everyone to see. The next day he was declared insolvent from the rostrum of the Exchange, and all NYSE members heard it announced that he had engaged in "conduct apparently contrary to just and equitable principles of trade."[40] He had stolen money from his partners and clubs to make margin calls. After years of funding his high living by using customer assets for himself and by stealing funds from the New York Yacht Club, where he was treasurer, Whitney surrendered to the authorities in 1938 and pled guilty to embezzlement.

It couldn't have made better newspaper copy: the man who had elegantly rebuffed the House's and Senate's accusations against the

Exchange was, himself, a crook. Whitney may have given the right answers to the committee, but his unusual circumstances played into the historical mistrust that both Washington and populist interests held for Wall Street. The most blue-blooded of the bunch turned out to be a thief. What more did the public need to discredit the practice of shorting?

The animus toward Whitney was so great that on April 12, 1938, when he was sent to Sing Sing prison, 5,000 people showed up to watch his departure from Grand Central Terminal in New York City. Leslie Gould, financial editor of the *New York Journal-American*, wrote that "the broker was the White Knight of the financial district. Whitney was Sir Richard when he went into battle in shining armor against the 1929 crash and again when he stood up and defied Washington and the reformers. Now it turns out that this Great White Knight was an optical illusion. . . ." [41] His comeuppance was the talk of gossip columnists.

CHAPTER 7

THE FIRST PRIME
BROKER WAS ACTUALLY
THE NYSE

Richard S. Whitney Before the House Judiciary Committee. The Committee
Representatives La Guardia, Michener, Tucker, Condon, Celler and

WHITNEY DENOUNCES LEGISLATION AIMED AT SHORT SELLING

Practice Is Essential to Maintaining a Stock Market, He Tells House Committee.

KEPT THE EXCHANGE OPEN

Government Regulation Would Mean a Breakdown in Efficiency, He Declares.

TRADING PROVIDES CHECKS

Shorts "Smooth the Waves, but Never Affect the Tides," He Says.

SPECIAL TO THE NEW YORK TIMES.

WASHINGTON, Feb. 24. — Short selling: is essential to the maintenance of stock exchanges, and stock exchanges are necessary to provide a market for investors. Richard Whitney, president of the New York Stock Exchange, told the House judiciary subcommittee, to day.

e of the making of the contract is . the owner or possessor of the urities sold."

he judiciary subcommittee, of ich Representative Tucker of rginia . . . . airman. listened . . . entiv . . . . 12,0 . . . ws. . . . lly . . . ar . . . s o . . . the . . . ve . . . th . . . no . . . ar . . . .

position because we w . . . could not carry out our matter of trust."

His summation of tl effect of short selling in market, under any cond that this practice "sn over affects . . .

short selling wo . . . the activities according to brok ers prefer a mar . can buy or sell at

Blow to Tradii
Barring of short crease the problem change firms, whose been reduced during years by the decrease tivity and the decli prices. Since their comm with the prices of sec decline of more than 70 the average of stock resulted in a large red these revenues. In Septem more than f . . . .

WALL ST. DISCUSSES SHORT STOCK SALES

Friends and Foes of Practice Agree a Law Against It Would Curtail Trading Sharply.

BROKERS' PROBLEMS CITED

With Business Reduced, Value of Memberships in Exchange Also Would Shrink.

Agitation in political and oth circles against short selling in tl securities markets has directed th attention of brokers to effects whic legislation against that practice would have on the volume of trad ng on the New York Stock xchange and on the value of mem erships in the Exchange.

The supporters and the foes of ort selling agree that any restric ons on that form of trading would sult in a sharp contraction of the siness done on the Exchange. ce the value of memberships tuates directly with the volume rading, a ban on short selling ld tend to reduce that valu ers? . . . .

SHORT SELLING OFTE A SUBJECT FOR DEBAT

"Bear" Operators, Censured by Pr dent Hoover, Have Stanch Defend as Well as Sharp Critics

BY EUGENE M. LOKEY.

THE public reaction to President Hoover's recent censure of "certain gentlemen" "who have been, selling short in the

ably, the short selling cont
Meanwhile, certain Sena Representatives in Congre manding legislative restr prevent the dislocation of

This system where traders and investment managers are
depositors of cash and collateral is called "prime brokerage."
It is the largest, most unnoticed banking system in the world.

The SEC rules that were passed in the 1930s are instructive for both what they addressed and what they did not. The decade ushered in major pieces of reform to end "the market abuses so common to the era." The reforms covered the setting of margin, laws for the new issuance of securities, passage of the Glass-Steagall Act, and registering the system's exchanges and securities—including the regulation of the NYSE and the regulation of short selling.[1]

Why did the NYSE fight so hard to make shorting the central element in its battle against regulation? Why had Whitney so vociferously defended the Exchange's acceptance of shorting? And why had his defense of shorting led to his post as the head of the Exchange? There were many issues that the Exchange and the Street could have fought over. But they picked shorting. Why? Because it had made them rich.

The reason the Exchange fought so hard over shorting was that the NYSE ran an early version of the modern prime brokerage business, one without regulation of haircuts, margin, or leverage. Prime brokerage is the business of clearing and settling trades, but it is also the banking system for all of today's hedge fund industry. A prime broker enables hedge funds to trade with many counterparts, while having their assets at one or two main prime brokers. The prime broker does everything for the funds. It clears trades, settles trades, and, most important, it provides leverage in the form of margin loans so the hedge fund can buy securities. The prime broker also lends securities to the short seller so that he can make delivery to the buyer.

In essence, the Exchange was a banking system that took deposits from its members and used that cash and collateral without having a clear compensation system for its members. The Exchange controlled the margin, interest rates, and free cash in a short transaction. The Exchange never had to report the amount of cash or collateral, and there were no uniform rules or protection against how much collateral the Exchange or its members had to secure on loans from their members or clients. There were no rules or protection regarding where and how they could use the proceeds. In a short-sale transaction, the short does not own anything except the cash he receives from the buyer. But the short seller must give the cash as collateral to the stock lender whose shares he delivers to the buyer.

This role must have given the Exchange an incredible amount of cash, since it could arbitrarily control how much excess collateral it could charge both to the lender and to the shorter of stock. For example, if I borrow a stock without giving any collateral to the lender—which many Exchange members unwittingly did—and lend that stock to a short seller, asking that he put up 25 percent margin, I just raised 125 percent of the value of the short sale at a very low interest rate. It was a way to act as a bank (deposit taker) without being a bank. The Exchange could take cash deposits, pay nothing for them, and relend or use the proceeds at a huge spread, one expanded by the Fed's interest hike during the early years of the Great Depression. This must have been a great offset to the volume slowdown caused by the crash of 1929. Volume dropped, but the ability of the Exchange to make interest income was a very good source of revenue in a very difficult market environment. This part of the Exchange's world was a system worth fighting for.

It was as if all the senators and congressmen were looking at the end of a flood pipe and complaining about the amount of water coming out. No one, it appears, sought to examine the width, depth, or construction of the pipe that brought the water. Then, as now, the mechanics and tools of how traders make markets and provide liquidity were seen as tools used by tradesmen and not worth the time of a real businessman. This knowledge never rose to the higher levels of the system, much as it often does not reach the level of portfolio manager or investment banker or deal maker today.

In this way, Wall Street has always been something of a caste system, where those dealing with higher mathematical models or maintaining board relationships often do not understand the foundation of the institutions whose credit they use for their clients. There is no real need to understand something that shows up at the door, something the staff—or the help, the thought goes—can prepare themselves. Even though the cost of short selling is intrinsic to almost every equity-trading strategy, no one seems to bother trying to understand the actual market mechanics of how short sellers conduct their business.

The raids, the intimidation, and the alleged conspiracy against shorting all focused on the effect of the short sale, not on the business of what happened after the trade was complete, or the relationship between the stock loan market, the cash market, and the liquidity it provided the dealer community. It never dawned on regulators that short-sale proceeds—the cash generated from a short-sale transaction that winds up in the hands of the person who lends the short stock—was a significant form of leverage. In fact, that leverage may have been a significant form of liquidity in the marketplace. But the early Exchange members knew they could use assets without securing those assets. Or, if they did secure them, they did so without overcollateralizing the loan. The resultant cash was therefore a pyramid of leverage. The government missed half the equation, and it was the half that, by far, meant the most economically to the institutions it wanted to regulate. The government wanted to regulate the sale part of the short sale, not the cash or financing part.

This system where traders and investment managers are depositors of cash and collateral is called "prime brokerage." It is the largest, most unnoticed, banking system in the world. The origins of this business came out of Whitney's testimony. Prime brokerage may be the only business on Wall Street where price transparency has actually marched backward with the disappearance of the Loan Crowd on the floor of the Exchange.

A prime broker's job is to give the investment manager the technology to book trades, record transactions, and settle those trades with its trading counterparts so that the manager can report his income statement to the investors. In return for giving the manager the technology to report his income statement, the manager gives the prime broker the use of his balance sheet and deposits the long positions, shorts, and cash with the bank. In enabling customers to trade with whomever they want, banks and broker dealers unlock a huge need for financing services for money managers who want the freedom to trade with many firms. The price of prime brokerage should be the credit risk incurred by the broker taking the risk of the party with whom the money manager trades. Why do they take this risk? Because it is one of the highest-margin businesses on Wall Street.

In essence, the money manager rents the operating system from the prime broker, leveraging off the clearance and settlement infrastructure already built by the broker, to run the books and records of his business. The prime broker is also a bank in the guise of a broker dealer. It takes custody of cash, securities, and short positions, and can, in most cases, use the collateral, cash, and economic standing of its clients for its own economic benefit. The prime broker uses its position as a custodian to do the same thing a bank does: take in deposits of cash and collateral and make a higher spread on the relending of its deposit base.

In assuming the risk of letting clients trade with whomever they want, whenever they want, the prime broker assumes the credit risk for settlement of the trades that the prime broker's customer did with other dealers, exchanges, and counterparties. There is no real published price for the cost of credit risk to clients for the prime broker to clear their trades. The cost of the exchange that the manager makes in hiring a prime broker—income statement reporting from the prime broker for depositing all cash and collateral to the prime broker—is supposed to be the equivalent of the credit risk taken by prime brokers to settle trades on behalf of their clients. The cost of the credit risk is nowhere near the profit spread the bank makes by using the relending of its deposits.

A big part of the profitability in prime brokerage is stock lending, which is a rather simple business in concept, but in its many uses becomes as complicated as any other trading business. In a stock loan transaction, the holder/owner of the security lends the stock to make delivery on a short sale. Because in a short sale the seller ends up owning cash, he sold something he doesn't own, and profits on the falling price of the stock (or losses in case the stock rises). In order to make delivery to the person who has bought the security, the short must deliver the securities that he borrowed. Stock is borrowed on an overnight basis. This means that, on any given day, the stock can be "recalled" from the seller, who may have to go into the open market to buy the stock sold in order to make delivery to the owner who lent it.

Stock lending is the lubricant to the business of arbitrage. Many of the new issuances of securities that Wall Street underwrites and distributes depend on the ability of buyers to hedge their risk (the entire convertible bond market, for example). Once you hear the word "hedge" in any equity transaction on Wall Street, odds are it involves the arrangement of stock lending. It is the easiest and most liquid way to conduct any number of trading strategies:

- To buy a target and sell the acquirer in merger arbitrage, you need to borrow stock.
- To buy a convertible bond and short the underlying common, you need to borrow stock.
- To short an underlying basket of stocks and buy the futures, you need to borrow stock.
- To hedge your option positions, you need to borrow stock.
- To go long distressed, high-yield, or bank loans, you probably need to borrow stock as delinquencies rise.

- To hedge the beta in your portfolio, you need to borrow stock.
- To participate in capital structure arbitrage, you need to borrow stock.
- To create a long-short portfolio, you need to borrow stock.
- To participate in the trading of American Depository Receipts, you need to borrow stock.

Stock borrowing is ubiquitous in the capital markets, and it is a market where price is allocated, not auctioned. This trillion-dollar, no-bid market is dominated by the largest prime brokers, agent banks, and insurance companies. The business of prime brokerage is still one of the few businesses in which big Wall Street firms will not disclose the money they make. It is *that* lucrative, even in spite of the recent turmoil and credit crisis–induced balance-sheet shrinkage.

During the 1920s and 1930s, just as now, the holders—the custodians—could use customer collateral in a way that was profitable to the custodian. In the early 1930s, accounts were not covered by the Securities Investment Protection Corporation (SIPC)—a government-sponsored insurance against failure or fraud now ubiquitously known on account of Bernie Madoff—so the brokers could use, without permission, the stock in a customer's account without necessarily posting collateral. This was like an interest-free loan by the customer to the broker. Regulators did not understand that by stepping on and squeezing the shorts, they were also constricting the funding structures of the firms. If a firm was dependent on the use of customer assets to fund it, then, like today, it was very easy to see why a CEO could say on Monday that everything was fine and still be broke by Friday. The reason Wall Street firms went under in 2008 was not because of shorting; it was because of their overreliance on short-term funding using prime brokerage assets as if they were real debt or equity issuances.

In a typical prime brokerage transaction, a client may put up 20 cents and borrow 80 cents to buy an asset worth a dollar. Using the 20 cents of customer margin as if it were capital is why Lehman and Bear Stearns failed. The value of stocks and bonds that make up the capital structure of a company may rise or fall, and with it, the leverage ratio of the company—but the money is permanent. Wall Street firms that used margin temporary money—in the example above, the 20 cents—as though it were permanent money found that once the firm's ability to pay its obligations comes into question, temporary money flees and leaves the firm scrambling to fund itself. One of the ways the firm does this is by selling what it already owns to bring down the balance sheet, thus ensuring that it has enough liquidity to meet its obligations. Once customer assets leave the door because the perceived credit exposure is too high for them, an unraveling can happen, sometimes in less than a week. Regulators in the 1920s and 1930s were blind to the fact that many of the firms used customer collateral to lend to short sellers; the firms controlled the cash generated from a short sale, cash that was a substitute form of financing for these firms. *By attacking the shorts and trying to help the equity price, regulators constricted the actual credit markets and funding sources that these firms needed for short-term liquidity to fund their operations.*

It was as if the regulators were unable to distinguish between those transactions that were directional in nature—a bet that the market will go up or down and that is not dependent on a spread—and those that were needed to hedge transactions to help companies expand their capital structures. Regulators lumped shorting into one bucket without understanding the implications of how money flows through our system.

Just as we today contemplate the reintroduction of the uptick rule and pursue rumormongering inquiries and restrictions on stock lending, the focus seems to be serving public opinion without serving the public. Shorting is, and was, a very intricate tool in our system. In the convertible bond market, for example, which is a huge source of debt for companies, the natural buyers are hedge funds that short stock to hedge their credit exposure. This is one of the many ways investors use shorting to get money into the hands of corporations.

To only address the uptick or stock-borrow rules is to tell the world we don't understand the market innovations of which we are so proud. Shorting can be expressed in so many different instruments that all we will do is chase down phantoms of rumors and waste time we do not have. CDS transactions can express a short, and short views can be expressed with over-the-counter puts, equity swaps, or a combination of option instruments that are either listed or over-the-counter, such as a reverse conversion. The point is that there are many listed and OTC options and futures strategies that can achieve the same economic purpose as shorting a stock. By saying that the fall of the stock market is caused by shorting is to "stand on top of a mountain and yell to the world, I don't understand the credit crisis and I don't want to."[2]

CHAPTER 8

THE SENATE TRIES AGAIN WITH THE PECORA COMMISSION

1932–1941

chard S. Whitney Before the House Judiciary Committee. The Committee ...
Representatives La Guardia, Michener, Tucker, Condon, Celler and ...

WHITNEY DENOUNCES LEGISLATION AIMED AT SHORT SELLING

Practice Is Essential to Maintaining a Stock Market, He Tells House Committee.

KEPT THE EXCHANGE OPEN

Government Regulation Would Mean a Breakdown in Efficiency, He Declares.

TRADING PROVIDES CHECKS

Shorts "Smooth the Waves, but Never Affect the Tides," He Says.

SPECIAL TO THE NEW YORK TIMES.

WASHINGTON, Feb. 24. — Short selling is essential to the maintenance of stock exchanges, and stock exchanges are necessary to provide a market for investors, Richard Whitney, president of the New York Stock Exchange, told a House judiciary subcommittee, to day.

... had been no short sellin

WALL ST. DISCUSSES SHORT STOCK SALES

Friends and Foes of Practice Agree a Law Against It Would Curtail Trading Sharply.

BROKERS' PROBLEMS CITED

With Business Reduced, Value of Memberships in Exchange Also Would Shrink.

Agitation in political and oth circles against short selling in th securities markets has directed th attention of brokers to effects which legislation against that practice would have on the volume of trading on the New York Stock xchange and on the value of memberships in the Exchange. The supporters and the foes of ort selling agree that any restric ns on that form of trading would ult in a sharp contraction of the iness done on the Exchange. e the value of memberships uates directly with the volume ading, a ban on short selling d tend to reduce that val

e of the making of the contract is the owner or possessor of the urities sold."

he judiciary subcommittee, of ch Representative Tucker of ginia ... ... man, listened enti ... 12,0 ws. ly ar ... s c the ve th o r

position because we w could not carry out our matter of trust."

His summation of th effect of short selling in market, under any cond that this practice "sn ... ver affects

short selling wo the activities according to brok ers prefer a mar can buy or sell at

Blow to Tradin Barring of short crease the problem change firms, whose been reduced during years by the decrease tivity and the decli prices. Since their comn with the prices of sec decline of more than 70 the average of stock l resulted in a large rec these revenues. In Septem more than f ...

SHORT SELLING OFTE A SUBJECT FOR DEBAT

"Bear" Operators, Censured by Pre dent Hoover, Have Stanch Defend as Well as Sharp Critics

BY EUGENE M. LOKEY.

THE public reaction to President Hoover's recent censure of "certain gentlemen" "who have been selling short in the

ably, the short selling conti Meanwhile, certain Sena Representatives in Congres manding legislative restri prevent the dislocation of

The day of the great promoter or the financial Titan,
to whom we granted everything if only he would build,
or develop, is over.

—Franklin Delano Roosevelt,
Commonwealth Club Address,
September 23, 1932, San Francisco

R ichard Whitney ended his 1932 Senate testimony with the following quote:

> Liquidation of securities, long selling, was a far more depressive force
> than short selling . . . Since the depression began, short selling
> accounted for less than 5 percent of exchange transactions . . . A pro-
> hibition of short selling would close markets and threaten the security
> of some bank loans in the amount of $5 billion . . . Recent market drops
> were in fact in the face of short covering . . . If there had been a sem-
> blance of a raid, then the Exchange would have stopped it as under its
> own constitution. They would have investigated those practices that
> demoralized the markets.[1]

Although the Senate Banking and Currency Committee moved
on after deciding that there was no evidence of a bear raid, that didn't

prevent further politicking. As intimated before, the committee was beleaguered by internal maneuvering. During the spring, Republican senators Walcott and Norbeck had jockeyed for power to set the committee agenda, with Senator Walcott of Connecticut establishing the bear-raid investigation when the committee chairman, Senator Norbeck of South Dakota, was out of town. Meanwhile, Senator Glass was actively pushing his own banking bill—the bill that would ultimately become the Glass-Steagall Act, which separated commercial and investment banking—through the committee. Since the hearings on short selling ultimately proved futile, and the monopolistic behavior of banks eventually became the committee's focus, Glass won out. The *New York Times* pointed out the disappointing results—or lack thereof—from the committee's hearings, reporting that "private conversations by members indicated that there was much chagrin over the negative results of an investigation that promised to yield 'sensational disclosures.'"[2]

The early part of the committee's testimony on bear raids, rumor-mongering, and short selling had gone the way of the early Pujo Committee, which is to say it went nowhere. Getting to the bottom of the evils of short selling had proved incredibly arduous. What the participants did was legal and permissible, and it was hard to make a case when the evidence was scarce and the only supposed crime was making money. So the senators involved in the investigation—perhaps mindful of how much press they received for subpoenaing the Rockefellers—decided to go after even bigger game: J. P. Morgan and the bank's "preferred list."

Sicily-born Ferdinand Pecora, a prominent New York attorney and judge, became the committee's chief counsel, a post he inherited almost by accident after the committee's previous special counsels either were fired or quit. (As a jab at Pecora's Mediterranean roots, the bankers termed the hearings the "Spanish Inquisition," highlighting the acrimony that exacerbated the relationship between Wall Street and Washington.) It was the Pecora Commission, as the Banking and Currency Committee came to be known, that found that trying to blame short selling for the crash was fruitless. It wanted bigger game. And thus from January 1933 to July 1934, the commission focused on J. P. Morgan's "preferred list" of approximately 500 people whom the bank viewed as important friends or clients—and sometimes both—and could be rewarded. To many people, the preferred list confirmed that Wall Street rigged the game and used money in the same way Tammany Hall used patronage: to generate credit when arms needed twisting. It confirmed Main Street's cynicism of Wall Street as being a place of loose ethics and easy riches.[3] According to Pecora, the men on the list were "primarily, men who were exceedingly eminent and powerful in finance, business, industry, politics, or public life."[4] In other words, they were just who the public might have expected.

One such man was William Woodin, the president of the American Car and Foundry Company, who would go on to serve as treasury secretary under Franklin Roosevelt. As an example of how the people on the list were rewarded, the commission presented a letter that a Morgan employee had sent to Woodin.[5]

I believe that the stock is selling in the market around $35 to $37 a share, which means very little, except that people wish to speculate. We are reserving for you 1,000 shares at $20 a share, if you would like to have it. There are no strings tied to this stock, and you can sell it whenever you wish . . . We just want you to know that we were thinking of you in this connection and thought you might like to have a little of the stock at the same price we are paying for it.[6]

But criticism over the preferred list was easy to defend. Why wouldn't an influential institution like J. P. Morgan turn to high-net-worth people who were willing to take risks and had an intelligible grasp of the marketplace? But the defense had its problems as well. The issue was that the list had the obvious and unshakable appearance of dishonesty. It also included influential people who took risks, including ex-presidents, former treasury secretaries, and other prominent citizens with potential for inside knowledge.[7]

Pecora said that the Morgan partners alone held 126 directorships in 89 corporations with total assets of $20 billion. "It was incomparably the greatest reach of power in private hands in our entire history," he noted. "It would be ridiculous to suppose, as sometimes has been asserted, that these indirect ties conferred on J. P. Morgan and Company [were] anything like control of all these thousands of additional corporations. But it would be equally fallacious to suppose that their intimate association with men who are apt to be leading members of the boards of these corporations did not exert a strong effect."[8]

The *Congressional Record* shows that a who's who of leading firms was called to testify. National City Bank and its investment affiliate, National City Company; J. P. Morgan and Co.; Kuhn, Loeb & Co.; Chase National Bank and its Chase Securities Corp.; Dillon, Read & Co.; Cities Service Co.; banking institutions in Detroit and Cleveland; and aviation companies. The records also contain completed questionnaires as part of the committee's investigation of the New York Stock Exchange, including 1,375 from Exchange members and special questionnaires for the Exchange itself.

The commission also began looking into the relationship between banking and securities affiliates, such as National City Bank and National City Company. It examined how depositors' money was being used in highly risky businesses. Charles Mitchell, the head of National City, received the blame for floating over $20 billion in new securities issues, many of them in the form of collateralized debt obligation of Latin American debt.[9] These were problematic because "the Company was sprung from the loins of the bank, derived from its initial capital from the surplus of the Bank, was owned by the same people, managed by the same people, and made perpetually indivisible the one from the other."[10]

The commission also looked at Chase president Albert Wiggin. Another easy target, Wiggin sat on 59 boards and shorted shares of Chase stock that earned several million dollars; the speculation was backed by an $8 million loan from Chase. He had also set up a Canadian securities company to avoid federal taxes.[11]

> *Pecora*: Do you think, Mr. Wiggin, it is a sound and ethical policy for a national bank to make loans to individuals among its officers or directors to enable those officers or directors, either individually or through the medium of private corporations, to engage in market activities in connection with the stock of the bank itself?
>
> *Wiggin*: I think so.[12]

Pecora was correctly implying that Wiggin and his cronies were manipulating the market with these loans to directors who could take advantage of their special relationship with the company and use privileged information. What forced Wiggin's resignation was not his short selling, but the circumstances of his short selling and all the other complaints Pecora collected against him. Nevertheless, to the public, short selling was once again associated with a crook. The news fell to notably receptive ears. Soon afterward, Winthrop Aldrich succeeded Wiggin at the helm of Chase and fought for the separation of commercial and investment banking to the mortification of his Wall Street compatriots.

Several other bigwigs were called down to testify, but even with Wiggin's illegal record, they managed to justify their profits to Pecora by demonstrating the enormous risks undertaken by their respective banks to generate those profits. (This technique is still used by Wall Street's top brass in order to defend outlandish executive compensation.)

REGULATION ARRIVES AS UPTICK, DOWNTICK

In the early 1930s, the president, the Senate, the House, and even the FBI began poring over Wall Street, looking for proof that speculators had not only brought the market down, but that they were keeping it down. Despite the lack of proof, the public and the government were convinced that short sellers were to blame. And the one thing that came out of the years of hearings was a new regulatory regime, which from 1930 to 1940 made several moves to hinder the shorts. FDR, who came to office in 1933, trumpeted the need for change, stating in his first inaugural address: "Practices of the unscrupulous money changers stand indicted in the court of public opinion, rejected by the hearts and minds of men,"[13]

FDR knew it was over for Richard Whitney and the Wall Street that acted as if it were the aristocracy of America. Roosevelt, however, *was* the very definition of a landed aristocrat, able to trace his lineage back to the *Mayflower*. His vitriolic contempt for Wall Street's perceived recklessness seemed to signal that Main Street's contempt was not merely a populist, or even bottom-up, movement—it had a leader who not only found himself inhabiting the highest seat in the land but also was a New

Yorker cut from the social fabric that the speculators themselves wished to emulate. Quoting again from FDR: "The day of the great promoter or the financial Titan, to whom we granted everything . . . is over."[14] Whitney had defended short sellers, the NYSE, and Wall Street practices, but FDR knew that he, a landed aristocrat himself, would have to put Wall Street back in its bottle. FDR was the Hamiltonian ideal of a member of the wealthiest class running the country, but with the wonderful irony of embracing Jefferson's disgust of a pseudo-aristocracy built on financial speculation.

In 1931, while Whitney's defense of shorting was being nationally broadcast, the government was beginning its initial foray into pressuring the New York Stock Exchange—which was regulated by the state of New York—to limit shorting. That year the NYSE introduced the "downtick," which deliberately impeded the practice of short selling. The rule gave buyers of securities the opportunity to sell their shares ahead of someone who had to borrow shares to sell stock. What lawmakers did not express—though it is unclear if the public would have even accepted it—is that the downtick rule was a direct attack on market liquidity. The crucial liquidity that shorts provided the marketplace was now being deterred.

The NYSE also issued the "uptick" rule, which states that a short sale cannot be executed at a price lower than the last sale. The clear goal was to keep bear raids from driving down stock prices "without impeding the functions of market makers."[15] The rule was introduced in the wake of Great Britain's abandonment of the gold standard, when the Exchange feared that the markets would not be able to open. It temporarily suspended short selling on September 21, 1931, and also required a daily short-interest report; five days later, on

September 26, all one-day shorting activity had to be reported to the Exchange.

On February 18, 1932, the Exchange passed another bureaucratic rule meant to cleverly—but not directly—impede shorting by attacking one of the steps required to pull it off. A law was passed mandating that stock lenders had to first receive permission in writing from the owners. So in order to make it difficult to borrow securities, and further hinder shorting, the Exchange put impediments in the borrowing process. Sound familiar? This is analogous to the locate procedures introduced in July 2008. Regulators tried to change the way people borrowed securities in a hope to curtail shorting activity. This was a way to try and crimp the short sellers by drying up the supply of shares that could be borrowed.

The Securities Exchange Act of 1934, the bill that created the SEC, gave the new commission the power to regulate short sales, but it also gave the Federal Reserve control over short-sale margins. Prior to the Fed regulating shorting, most of it was done on 25 percent margin as compared to the 50 percent set by the Fed.

The SEC, in 1935, also established an uptick rule (it had actually been introduced in the 1934 act), which stated that a short sale could not be executed unless the previous trade was completed at a higher price. There were, as it turned out, many unintended consequences that required a rejiggering of the uptick rule. The SEC had not understood the law of unintended consequences and had to adjust the rule for the hedging requirements of warrant traders and the downtick needs of regional exchanges that needed to bring "that market's price in line with the primary market's price."[16]

In 1937, amid another market rout, the subject of bear raids again found its way onto the radar of both the public and Washington. What the SEC discovered in its investigation was similar to what it would later find in the Pollack Report of 1989, which investigated shorting practices. It unearthed, according to the research of Charles M. Jones, "that short sales were a small part of total sales during the decline, but there was concentrated shorting by a small number of Exchange members in certain stocks in certain times . . . on October 5, [1937], when prices were stabilizing after a sharp intraday decline, floor trades arrived with orders to short 2,700 shares of US Steel, about 20% of the stock's average daily volume. The Commission was concerned that 'public support of US Steel at this level could not withstand this concerted assault.'"[17] Furthermore, it found what we know today: that the other 80 percent of the volume was either long selling or buying. Prices declined because of an absence of bids, not because of a colluding cabal that drove prices down.

For over 300 years—from as early as when the Dutch East India Company protested to the Amsterdam Stock Exchange about the large profits made by short sellers—regulators have struggled to balance the interests of buyers and sellers. During the prolonged downturn in the markets during the 1930s, there was a consistent story. When price discovery was one way—up—then pessimists had no chance to participate in the markets and were effectively shut out. "When arbitrage opportunities are limited by allowing optimistic agents to have an unfair influence on prices, pessimists are effectively shut out of the markets, and prices can be set by optimists (agents with high valuations)."[18]

During President Hoover's term in office, the NYSE was pressured to discourage shorting, and the Exchange quietly but firmly asked its members to not lend stock in order to shrink the supply available to short. There were FBI investigations into rumormongering and a perceived threat of legal prosecution against those who shorted. The uptick rule went further, discouraging and limiting shorting.

Naturally, in this environment of hysteria, prices "adjust more slowly to new negative information. As a result of this slower adjustment, market makers tend to lose more to the remaining informed traders. In order to protect themselves from these informed traders, market makers must set wider bid-ask spreads."[19]

Liquidity dried up as market makers who did not see short order flow were exposed to more risk. Ultimately, this shrunk trading volume and discouraged market participation as the bid-ask spread skyrocketed. The request for verification that the lender of his securities was aware that they were being borrowed was a price shock to the securities lending market.

> The price of shorting went up at the beginning of April 1932, and the quantity of shorting fell sharply as well . . . the cost of maintaining a short position rose considerably at the start of April . . . some shorts decided to exit their positions or avoid taking new ones.[20]

The shock was not one of price, but that floor brokers who could once borrow stock for free defended their spread through passed-on cost. The reaction was the same then as it is today: find an arcane way to limit shorting rather than address how to make the marketplace fair for both sides.

The written authorization rule led to higher premiums for borrowing stock, but "these premiums did not last for long, however, as the price system worked its usual magic. High lending fees made more shares available for lending. The increase in the cost of shorting induced many to cover their shorts, reducing shorting demand. Within two weeks, conditions in the securities lending market had returned to normal."[21]

The problem with the short sellers was that they were perceived as the antagonist thwarting Frederick Jackson Turner and Williams Jennings Bryan's monocausal view of the world. They represented the one financial instrument that could explain away the destructive effects of trusts, corporations, and holding companies without the fear of attacking an owner of production or landed stakeholder. Squeezing, attacking, regulating, outing, and skewering the shorts was attractive and facilitated by the fact that they have no legal standing; they do not own anything, other than cash proceeds from the short sale, and they don't parley with boards of directors.

Shorts are not traditional stakeholders, and their economic strategy is very straightforward: stocks fall, and the shareholder, employee, and management suffer while speculators—whom many imagine to be all-powerful and manipulative—profit. There are no interlocking directorships, complicated financial products, or financial systems to explain. Only the asymmetric, zero-sum nature of shorting needs to be understood to attack it. Short selling had been discouraged, but the association of concentrated power and seemingly seamy wealth made speculators and the firms that shorted stocks on Wall Street an easy target for the New Deal. "Step by step the stockholder is being disenfranchised" by the coordination of trade or industrywide coordinating groups, which was more subtle but just as effective as some of the trusts that previous committees/commissions were looking for.[22]

The NYSE went after short selling to protect itself from federal regulation, and the Exchange's chief defender was the not yet disgraced Dick Whitney. "The New York Stock Exchange, a leader in the attempt to defeat securities legislation, took an even more active part as the unrelenting spearhead of opposition to legislation regulating the stock exchanges of the nation."[23]

The NYSE did not immediately accept the idea of regulation. In fact, the Exchange fought it. Hard. Early in 1934, after facing down many of the senators now calling for regulation of not only short sales but also the entire Exchange, Whitney called the Exchange a "'perfect institution'—and rejected the idea that the government should regulate the securities business."[24] This was just as it is today, with Wall Street fighting a Federal Reserve and Treasury move to federally regulate Exchange-cleared and Exchange-traded products for credit default swaps—an insurance product with no clear, outright regulator—to protect profits and margin. Also like today, an investigation into short selling had produced little except Washington chasing the same old phantom of rumormongering and trying to define abusive short selling.

A clear pattern emerged from the congressional investigations of shorting in the 1930s. But the investigations into the machinations of Wall Street's leading firms were legitimate, so the government saw an opening to expand federal power with the creation of the Securities and Exchange Commission in 1934, which gave it regulatory power over much of the capital markets. One way to get Wall Street off balance enough for the government to stick a regulatory nose into the tent was by stoking the public's emotion over shorting.

FDR handed the commisson over to Joseph Kennedy, the famous speculator and bootlegger, who saw to it that finance would not be driven by the head of the NYSE or 23 Wall Street, but by federal fiat. He understood that private financial influence would ebb and regulatory control would flourish.

Kennedy represented what both Hamilton and Jefferson feared in the moneyed elite. Jefferson feared that the moneyed interest would be counterrevolutionaries, would betray the ideals of the republic, and would become seduced by the ideas of strong, central government, or worse, monarchy. Hamilton thought that the financial aristocracy was disengaged from power enough to understand its social responsibility not to abuse the ultimate power given to it in the name of the republic. Kennedy, as SEC chairman, would certainly not be disengaged from power. Originally, his appointment was thought of as a joke, but the poacher-turned-gamekeeper proved those fears unwarranted as he presided over the introduction of the most sweeping securities regulation in America's history.

Kennedy got his job even though he was a financial operator himself. He had participated in the Libby-Owens Ford stock pool, creating an artificially low supply of the stock to goose the price. The pool, which made Kennedy a very rich man, was like so many others—investigated by Ferdinand Pecora, who would later report to Kennedy at the SEC.

Amid all the scrutiny from the Judiciary and Senate Banking Committees, Kennedy had performed something of a Talleyrand, the French diplomat who changed sides five times during the French Revolution, only to come out with a more elite perch each time. Kennedy was never called in front of either committee, even though he was an incredibly well-known speculator. He was certainly behind many market schemes both long and short, but his business activities of the 1930s are almost impossible to construct.

Accounts of the Libby Owens Ford pool's actions [and Joseph Kennedy's participation in them] survive largely because they had been scrutinized and recorded as part of the Senate Banking and Currency Committee's investigations into stock exchange practices at the time.

Whatever his other contemporaneous securities interests and trading practices may have been, having escaped public notice at the time, they remain obscure. Almost no mention survives of letters among Joe Kennedy's papers beyond a few passing references to the committee's chief counsel, Ferdinand Pecora.[25]

After Kennedy took office, he explained that the new rules were "simple and honest. Only those who see things crookedly will find them harsh."[26] But Kennedy's tenure as chairman was over by the time a recession hit hard again in late 1937, undermining the New Deal's prospects at success and reigniting public discontent.

As another wave of panic hit in 1937, the public clamored for another round of trials, another wave of investigations, more justice, and, perhaps, more names. The Whitney scandal played no small part in creating this public appetite, as did FDR's political rhetoric. Roosevelt labeled bankers, speculators, and short sellers "economic royalists," a loaded term that harkened back to populist critiques of moneyed trusts, or, even further back, to a form of unforgivable anti-Revolutionary sentiment. In June of 1938, FDR convened a joint executive-congressional Temporary National Economic Committee (TNEC) to decide the best course of action.

The public was in an angry mood. Many people had decided the bankers were responsible for their losses, and the conviction that thousands of innocent investors had been mulcted by self-serving financiers was strengthened still further by various congressional hearings, which almost daily disclosed new evidence of financial negligence, irresponsibility, and favoritism."[27]

The TNEC broke the scale for government investigations, making quick history of the already elaborate Pecora Commission. Upon the TNEC's closing in 1941, the committee had spent over $1 million, hired a 182-person staff of experts, explored 95 different industries, heard 552 witnesses, left 37 volumes of printed testimony, and produced 43 documentary monographs.[28] The debate largely circled around the new economic doctrines of a British economist named John Maynard Keynes, who saw "compensatory" deficit spending as the way out of the economic mess. In his 1936 treatise *The General Theory of Employment, Interest, and Money*, Keynes argued that borrowing money for government spending (while leading to a deficit) could "prime the pump" for economic recovery. In other words, a little government spending on credit could trigger much larger private spending and bring the federal government out of the red. To orthodox economists, the suggestion—trading government deficits for economic recovery—seemed outrageous.[29] For the New Dealer, the natural solution was another round of antitrust regulation to break up the alleged monopolies. But despite the widespread antitrust sentiment, war industrialization during 1941 made antitrust efforts seem divisive and an impediment to economic recovery.

As prolific as the TNEC was, the country's mobilization for war overshadowed the entire debate. The economy seemed to be improving, and the vigorously defended policy positions of economic wonks and senior statesmen were quickly forgotten. A 1941 *Time* article eulogized that, "with all the ammunition the committee had stored up, a terrific broadside might have been expected. Instead, the committee rolled a rusty BB gun into place [and] pinged at the nation's economic problems."[30]

Of the many things TNEC did not accomplish, it most certainly did not provide the U.S. government its precise case against Wall Street. Previous investigations invoked needed reforms and exposed white-collar criminals, but the uneasiness felt toward Wall Street persisted. Part of the reason was that the generation of New Dealers who arrived for Roosevelt's first administration and were now firmly established in powerful positions bonded over this distrust of capitalism. As historian David Kennedy observes: "Though [New Dealers] represented a broad range of opinions and sometimes clashed over specific policies, they shared certain core beliefs: a deep suspicion of businessmen and a fierce faith in government as the agency of justice and progress."[31] One monopoly that the TNEC did see put under federal jurisdiction was the NYSE. With the TNEC in session, the stock market reeling, and Whitney having been arrested, the third SEC chairman, William O. Douglas (who would go on to become a Supreme Court justice), was at last able "to compel the NYSE to democratize its board and adopt short-sale trading rules."[32]

And so in 1947, the U.S. Attorney's office filed suit against 17 investment banks and the Investment Banking Association (IBA) for violation of the Sherman Antitrust Act, in hopes of finally bringing Wall Street to its knees. The case was *United States v. Henry S. Morgan et al.*, and it would last for six years.

CHAPTER 9

UNITED STATES V. HENRY S. MORGAN

1947–1953

hard S. Whitney Before the House Judiciary Committee. The Committee...
Representatives La Guardia, Michener, Tucker, Condon, Celler and...

brought down a fresh
e upon the heads of
d professional oper-
been profiting by the
ne in wheat prices. It
t of a novelty to have
oin in the rising cho-
ation, but the specu-
hood seem...

undermi
finger up
speculat
erning a
commodi
have lon
only with
Th

WHITNEY DENOUNCES LEGISLATION AIMED AT SHORT SELLING

Practice Is Essential to Maintaining a Stock Market, He Tells House Committee.

KEPT THE EXCHANGE OPEN

Government Regulation Would Mean a Breakdown in Efficiency, He Declares.

TRADING PROVIDES CHECKS

Shorts "Smooth the Waves, but Never Affect the Tides," He Says.

SPECIAL TO THE NEW YORK TIMES.

WASHINGTON, Feb. 24. — Short
selling: is essential to the maintenance of stock exchanges, and
stock exchanges are necessary to
provide a market for investors,
Richard Whitney, president of the
New York Stock Exchange, told the
House judiciary subcommittee, today.

...there had been no short sellin

from mi
over sto
outright
of whic
Mr.
the su
been
year
Excha
disco
short
Re
whic
said
to f
will
con
par
late
pos

of
th
s

of the making of the contract is
the owner or possessor of the
urities sold."

he judiciary subcommittee, of
ch Representative Tucker of
ginia... irman, listened
enti... 12,0...
ws.
ly
ard
s o
the
re
th
ov
ry

position because we w
could not carry out our
matter of trust."

His summation of th
effect of short selling in
market, under any cond
that this practice "sn
...ver affects

short selling wo
the activities
according to brok
ers prefer a mar
can buy or sell at

WALL ST. DISCUSSES SHORT STOCK SALES

Friends and Foes of Practice Agree a Law Against It Would Curtail Trading Sharply.

BROKERS' PROBLEMS CITED

With Business Reduced, Value of Memberships in Exchange Also Would Shrink.

Agitation in political and oth
circles against short selling in th
securities markets has directed th
attention of brokers to effects whic
legislation against that practice
would have on the volume of trad-
ng on the New York Stock
xchange and on the value of mem-
erships in the Exchange.
The supporters and the foes of
ort selling agree that any restric-
ns on that form of trading would
ult in a sharp contraction of the
iness done on the Exchange.
ce the value of memberships
tuates directly with the volume
ading, a ban on short selling
d tend to redu...

Blow to Tradi
Barring of short
crease the problem
change firms, whose
been reduced during
years by the decrease
tivity and the decli
prices. Since their comn
with the prices of sec
decline of more than 70
the average of stock
resulted in a large red
these revenues. In Septem
more than f...

SHORT SELLING OFTE[N] A SUBJECT FOR DEBAT[E]

"Bear" Operators, Censured by Pre[si]dent Hoover, Have Stanch Defende[rs] as Well as Sharp Critics

By EUGENE M. LOKEY.

THE public reaction to President Hoover's recent censure
of "certain gentlemen" who
...selling short in the

ably, the short selling conti
Meanwhile, certain Sena
Representatives in Congress
manding legislative restri
prevent the dislocation of

I have come to the settled conviction and accordingly find that no such combination, conspiracy and agreement was ever made, entered into, conceived, constructed, continued or participated in by these defendants.

—JUDGE HAROLD MEDINA,
SEPTEMBER 1953

For over 40 years, the government had failed to prove its case— whether it was the Pujo Committee, the Pecora Commission, or the TNEC. The accusation was that Wall Street harbored a cabal of moneyed trusts, a shady group of insiders who plotted to make themselves rich at the expense of others. After World War II the government tried again, this time with the granddaddy of all its efforts. In 1947, the Justice Department brought a case for collusion against Henry S. Morgan, the son of J. P. Morgan, Jr., and the head of Morgan Stanley and 17 other investment banks on the Street.

The case asserted what many in and out of government had long believed—that Wall Street was an old boys club where power and information was shared in some sort of equation that proffered money to the chosen at the expense of the unchosen. The Justice Department filed an antitrust case against the investment banks and the Investment

Banking Association for violating the Sherman Antitrust Act. The government said there was "an integrated, overall conspiracy and combination formed in or about 1915 and in continuous operation thereafter, by which the defendants as a group developed a system to eliminate competition and monopolize the cream of the business of investment banking."[1]

A *Wall Street Journal* article in October 1947 mentioned that 69 percent of all securities were underwritten by the 17 firms mentioned in the case, Morgan Stanley, Lehman Brothers, Goldman Sachs, First Boston, and Kuhn, Loeb among them. The case centered on the degree of competitiveness in the bidding of securities. The consensus was that Truman, like FDR, would want to pursue the TNEC's unfinished probe into the concentration of private corporate power. The government wanted to show how the syndicates excluded smaller investment banks while keeping the majority of the business for themselves.

Most of the investment banks seemed to split industry coverage among themselves. General Motors was a Morgan client, for example; Ford was with Goldman, and so on. It was something of a gentleman's game, where poaching accounts was forbidden. Since firms had such deep relationships with certain companies, it was the equivalent of an exclusive arrangement with certain accounts. All the banker had to do was execute what the client wanted and the banker stood a good chance of getting all of the client's advisory and underwriting assignments. The idea was that by breaking the relationship between "traditional bankers" and the corporate clients, the bidding process would open up to other large public investors.[2]

Many on Wall Street complained that there was no auction process to get the business, and that underwriting syndicates had agreed not to poach among themselves. Some firms, such as Merrill, Lazard, and Salomon Brothers, were sympathetic to the suit and tried to help the Justice Department make its case. They wanted to see more competitive bidding for new issues and for industry sectors like railroads and public utilities, which seemingly were handled by the same firms year after year with little or no price discovery by the issuer.[3] Issuing companies accepted that the price they were being charged to raise capital was the best price. Companies did not shop around to get the lowest fees and cheapest funds. The process favored the incumbent banker.

The Justice Department's position was that "over the years, the top Wall Street firms maintained a hold on their businesses through the use of syndicates where only other banks invited could help underwrite a new security issue. Proof of those syndicates had excluded smaller investment banks . . . while keeping the lion's share of the business for themselves was evidence of monopoly concentration."[4] The defense claimed, however, that the naturally high barrier of capital that needed to be committed to the long-standing relationships explained the lack of new entrants into the business. It was exclusive in that it discriminated against those unwilling to put their money at risk to support their clients. The government charged that there was a remarkable similarity in the firms that dominated the underwriting of securities, and that the pattern of who won the business was not a random competitive process.

The trial did not open until 1950, because it took more than three years to gather testimony and witnesses. Wall Street understood the stakes; it had seen this line of attack before, so it gathered a lot of resources to defend itself.

But Wall Street was not the behemoth it had been. These firms were so small that they did not have $5 million in capital among them.[5] The investment banks were smaller, spun-out versions of their Depression-era parent banking operations: J. P. Morgan, Chase, and National City. As Ron Chernow wrote in his book, *The House of Morgan*, "If one added up the combined capital of Morgan Stanley and the next seven investment banks, together they were only a third the size of Chase and National City securities affiliates of 1929."[6]

In September 1953, after ruling two years previously that no evidence prior to 1935 was permissible, Judge Harold Medina dismissed the Justice Department's case without hearing the defense. Medina never got a satisfactory answer from the prosecution as to why the rankings of the underwriting firms moved around so much. Some firms moved up the ranks and then down. If their actions were to be collusive, why then would firms bother to change places? The firms would move on a much more predictable basis and rotate positions, and in that way share the wealth of the syndicate. Medina also saw that one firm was at the top of the tables, and that was Morgan Stanley. It defied logic that the lead runner would always be the same firm if there were collusion among the participants.[7] Medina observed that it was illogical for a fixed and rigged system to always have interchanging parts. He observed that competition among the firms in the case was intense and that firms occupied different rankings over the time in question. This undermined the idea that the system was uncompetitive.

The government, not without some logic, argued that the firms were nothing but the continuation of pre–Glass-Steagall Wall Street, where Morgan Stanley, the investment bank, was just the extension of Morgan, the bank.

Medina found this line of reasoning implausible. "I have come to the settled conviction and accordingly find that no such combination, conspiracy and agreement was ever made, entered into, conceived, constructed, continued or participated in by these defendants," he said.[8] He blamed the government for bringing a spurious assault against Wall Street, for "chasing a phantom conspiracy constructed from flimsy circumstantial evidence."[9] He barred the government from bringing any similar litigation against the banks in the future.

Even though the Morgan case began under Truman's administration and ended during Eisenhower's tenure—two presidents, it should be noted, with very different approaches to business—it was a continuation of the long search for the financial bogeyman that destroyed a generation of wealth in the 1930s. The "government's allegations were motivated by prejudice, faulty evidence, lack of knowledge, and a combination of all three."[10] The case cost the defense $7.5 million while the government spent $3 million. Eleven law firms were involved, with 45 lawyers for the defense and 12 for the prosecution.

The populist passion for prosecuting Wall Street ended with the Medina case. Underwriting was the main business of Wall Street at the time. It is hard to see investment banking, given its current product depth and complexity, being dominated by a syndicate when half of the members did not have $5 million in capital between them. For the rest of the century, federal authorities would bring cases against Wall Street that would target certain behavior and segments of the industry—insider trading, preferred lists, research for banking scandals—but would never wholly challenge the Street's raison d'etre. In the Morgan case, underwriting was what defined Wall Street. Wall Street investment banks, from the time of Medina's decision on, would attempt to reunite with commercial banks to look like the institutions that existed before Glass-Steagall was enacted.

The $1 billion bear-raid headlines of April 1932 proved more ferocious and more titillating than a complicated trial about underwriting. The actual boredom of investment banking had inspired Ralph Carson, an attorney at Davis Polk, which was defending Morgan Stanley, to say that the trial was a "Sahara of words."[11] Wall Street just wasn't that exciting anymore, and finally, a couple of decades after the initial short-sale hearings, the public passion to make Wall Street pay for its past sins faded away.

CHAPTER 10

YESTERDAY AS THE DAY BEFORE

1987–Present

Richard S. Whitney Before the House Judiciary Committee. The Committee [...] Representatives La Guardia, Michener, Tucker, Condon, Celler and [...]

WHITNEY DENOUNCES LEGISLATION AIMED AT SHORT SELLING

Practice Is Essential to Maintaining a Stock Market, He Tells House Committee.

KEPT THE EXCHANGE OPEN

Government Regulation Would Mean a Breakdown in Efficiency, He Declares.

TRADING PROVIDES CHECKS

Shorts "Smooth the Waves, but Never Affect the Tides," He Says.

SPECIAL TO THE NEW YORK TIMES.

WASHINGTON, Feb. 24. — Short selling is essential to the maintenance of stock exchanges, and stock exchanges are necessary to provide a market for investors, Richard Whitney, president of the New York Stock Exchange, told the House judiciary subcommittee, to day.

[...] had been no short selli[ng]

WALL ST. DISCUSSES SHORT STOCK SALES

Friends and Foes of Practice Agree a Law Against It Would Curtail Trading Sharply.

BROKERS' PROBLEMS CITED

With Business Reduced, Value of Memberships in Exchange Also Would Shrink.

Agitation in political and oth[er] circles against short selling in th[e] securities markets has directed th[e] attention of brokers to effects which legislation against that practice would have on the volume of trading on the New York Stock Exchange and on the value of memberships in the Exchange.

The supporters and the foes of short selling agree that any restrictions on that form of trading would result in a sharp contraction of the business done on the Exchange. [Si]nce the value of memberships [flu]ctuates directly with the volume [of] trading, a ban on short selling [wo]uld tend to reduce that value [bro]kers? belie[ve]

[...]ne of the making of the contract is [... a]t the owner or possessor of the [se]curities sold."

The judiciary subcommittee, of [w]hich Representative Tucker of [V]irginia [... chair]man, listened [at]tentive[ly ...] 12,0[...] [vi]ews, [...] [u]ally [Gu]ard [was o...] [i]s the [gi]ve [au]th [sho]w [sa]r[...]

position because we w[...] could not carry out our [...] matter of trust."

His summation of th[e] effect of short selling i[n the] market, under any con[ditions] that this practice "sn[...] [...] never affects [...]

short selling wo[uld ...] the activities [...] according to brok[...] ers prefer a mar[ket ...] can buy or sell at [...]

Blow to Tradi[ng]

Barring of short [selling ...] crease the problem[...] change firms, whose [...] been reduced during [recent] years by the decrease [in ac]tivity and the decli[ne in] prices. Since their comm[issions vary] with the prices of sec[urities, the] decline of more than 70 [... in] the average of stock [prices] resulted in a large red[uction in] these revenues. In Septem[ber ...] more than f[...]

SHORT SELLING OFTE[N] A SUBJECT FOR DEBAT[E]

"Bear" Operators, Censured by Pr[esi]dent Hoover, Have Stanch Defend[ers] as Well as Sharp Critics

BY EUGENE M. LOKEY.

THE public reaction to President Hoover's recent censure of "certain gentlemen" "who have been selling short in the [...]

[...]ably, the short selling con[...] Meanwhile, certain Sen[ators and] Representatives in Congre[ss de]manding legislative restr[...] prevent the dislocation o[f ...]

[...] upon the heads of [...]d professional oper[ators ... have] been profiting by the [decli]ne in wheat prices. It [...] of a novelty to have [... j]oin in the rising cho[...] [specul]ation, but the specu[...] [neighbor]hood seem[s ...]

from [...] over s[...] outrigh[t ...] of wh[...]

Mr[...] the s[...] been [...] year[s ...] Exc[hange ...] disc[...] sho[...]

[...] wh[...] sai[d ...] to [...] wi[...] co[...] p[...] la[...] p[...]

finger [...] specula[tion ...] erning [...] commo[...] have l[...] only w[...]

Th[...]

*I don't want to penalize people for enterprising and discover-
ing information on their own and using it themselves, and I
don't think our law should be designed to prohibit that in
any way. I wouldn't think you would either.*

—CHRISTOPHER COX, REPUBLICAN
CONGRESSMAN FROM CALIFORNIA, 1989

The Henry S. Morgan case represented the government's last great
attempt to discipline and control Wall Street until the 1980s. But
in 1989, two years after Black Monday, Congress took another shot at
short selling. The Commerce, Consumer, and Monetary Affairs Subcommittee of the House Committee on Government Operations held
a hearing on "Short-Selling Activity in the Stock Market: The Effects
on Small Companies and the Need for Regulation." The subcommittee took three days—and almost 1,000 pages—of testimony, with
many government, Exchange, and industry representatives testifying
about short selling.

This subcommittee would have been just a minor footnote in the
history of Washington's long battle with Wall Street were it not for the
participation of one panel member and the position he took: Christopher Cox, who sat on the subcommittee as a Republican congressman

from California. In 2005, he would become the chairman of the Securities and Exchange Commission under President George W. Bush. The subcommittee started the row by considering more rules to curb short selling. And in 1989, Cox took on Whitney's mantle and actually defended the shorts. Two decades later, he would take a decidedly different position.

The subcommittee's hearing was shrouded in shades of the past. In fact, reading the testimony is like experiencing déjà vu. Just as Frank Parish had accused Standard Oil of bear raiding his Missouri-Kansas's stock, chief executives of small companies complained about bear raids. Big Wall Street houses testified, as did the NASD, the SEC, and the NYSE. The executives claimed that the shorts were in league with journalists, investors, and insiders; they were bent on destroying the companies' stock prices through bear raids and naked shorting. They called for an uptick rule for the OTC and NASD. Although no one attempted to satisfactorily define short selling, congressmen such as Dennis Hastert, a Republican from Illinois, said that abusive shorting should be prosecuted. The politicians seemed to treat the short sellers like a great political piñata. Since the short sellers did not testify in person, but rather had letters read into the record, the politicians could just heap invective on them. The shorts would not even come to Congress to defend themselves. It took Cox to do that, and even the SEC's testimony defended shorting.

The 1989 hearings made clear how technological advancement had rolled back the clock on Wall Street behavior. Firms could now settle trades electronically, which allowed them to mimic the bad business practices—including the borrowing and lending of customers' assets without their permission—that the Whitney hearings had discussed. The subcommittee's principal contention was that naked shorting was the main culprit for bear raids. The Wall Street experts whom Congress asked to testify maintained that it was impossible to police shorting, and in particular, naked shorting. The reason was that the Depository Trust Company—the central clearing and depository mechanism for trading on Wall Street—allowed collateral to be used interchangeably, making it fungible across all brokerages. The new clearing technology and arrangements at the Depository Trust Company, where all the short positions were held in the name of the bank or investment bank and not in the name of the owner, enabled the Street to collude with short sellers so they could sell stock without making delivery.

The experts charged that since the Street settled on a net basis, firms either overlent the shares that they had held in the Depository Trust Company or they lent to the shorts fully-paid-for stock that was not held in Street name without the customer's permission. Customer assets were being used without their owners' consent or knowledge to enable short-sale transactions.

However, what the brokerage executives recommended was in fact dysfunctional. Essentially, they wanted all accounts, no matter the size, to be able to tell the banks that held their assets where to put those assets. They wanted to disaggregate the clearance function that made more trading, and the development of other markets, possible. It was the equivalent of putting your money into a bank and then dictating that the bank could lend your money only to certain institutions. Executives also debated the introduction of the uptick rule, whether or not short sellers should have to identify themselves in a filing with the SEC, and the extent to which the filing should apply to the short seller.

The testimony of Robert Spira, the chairman of Berkeley Securities, and John Flaherty, president of the OTC Newsletter, centered on naked shorting and claims of shorts engaging in rumormongering. Senior officers of Carrington Laboratories, IGI, and American City Business Journal complained in their testimony, just as Parish had, that short sellers had conducted bear raids and were passing false information. "Shorts have repeatedly maliciously intervened in the administration and financing of our company and have attempted to frustrate our research. They have contacted Government agencies who regulate us, the SEC and the FDA specifically, stockholders, and our research consultants and their employees. Short sellers have exerted enormous effort to discredit us with these people upon whom the success of our business depends."[1]

These executives argued that naked shorting was the equivalent of issuing new shares. Thus, they said, short sellers should be required to make the same representations that an issuer does. Shorts would have to issue their own disclosures to the SEC to ensure that the shorts' research was publicly available.

The companies' executives and some executives from small-tier brokerages argued that short selling unfairly interfered with the financing of their companies. The emerging Japanese economy, they argued, was killing the United States because Japan did not allow shorting. The companies' chiefs said that bear raids were common in their OTC markets and that short sellers were in league with Barron's and other publications to disseminate false information and then trade on the result. The executives said that this so-called prepublication trading was the result of collusion between a press that favored the shorts and short sellers who loved to get a position in a stock before the story—which they presumably leaked—was published. This was when Christopher Cox stepped in:

I really want to focus on the civil side of this, but using as a . . . paradigm the sort of Perry Mason model where you have lawyers for defendants and you have lawyers for the prosecution and they are each in there telling very different stories . . . the jury gets to make up its mind about who is telling the truth, and isn't that the way we want the marketplace to work? Don't we want companies that are putting out lots of rosy information about their prospects to have that information tempered by people who have a financial interest, just like people that own shares going up, by people who have a financial interest in making them go down. That it is what we call a level playing field. We put out information that is rosy, and the blemishes of the company we can rely on the marketplace to expose. If we followed that model, why wouldn't we expect that the system would self-police. If I sue the company because my shares have gone down, I file a 10b-5 lawsuit. Why wouldn't the company, if the company were in fact telling the truth and short sellers were spreading bad rumors, pull the short sellers in the lawsuit and redress against them.[2]

Flaherty answered by saying many of the companies that short sellers targeted were weak and frequently had suits filed against them by shareholders. Those suits made it difficult for the companies to divulge information to defend themselves against the shorts because it would spill over into the lawsuits. The cost and time that a case would require also made a lawsuit logistically and financially infeasible.

"But if we have a rule that says it [spreading false rumors and then shorting stocks] is illegal already and we have people breaking the rules, aren't we left to having to enforce those rules?"[3] Cox asked. "The court system is all we have."[4]

"I am not sure exactly what is illegal and what is not illegal in these bear raids," Flaherty said.[5] "I have never seen it spelled out."[6]

"Every single example you have given about . . . spreading false rumors is already illegal," Cox said.[7]

"Is prepublication trading before an article illegal?" Flaherty asked.[8]

"If it is based on material nonpublic information, certainly it is insider trading."[9]

"I don't know," Flaherty said.[10]

"If it is not, it is news to me . . . in that sense, I don't think the rules are any different whether you are long or short," Cox said.[11]

What Cox said was that the way corporations should settle their issues with the shorts was not to ban the activity, but for those corporations to sue the short sellers and let a jury decide. To put a fine point on this: 20 years ago, when the market capitalization of the small and mid-size companies was, indeed, small, due process was suggested as a just solution to complaints about short selling; 20 years later, when the companies that complain about short selling are capitalized in the billions (when they are, indeed, some of the world's most recognizable financial institutions), due process is not appropriate for large enterprises. Instead, it was determined in the fall of 2008 that the practice of shorting financial stocks should be done away with and banned.

The testimony then turned to the arguments of disclosure. The way Congress handled disclosure in the 1932 hearings was to leak the identity of the shorts to the *New York Times* and shame them into stopping. Flaherty and Spira said the shorts should be forced to make a filing similar to a 13d filing, where long investors have to declare to the SEC when they own over 5 percent of a company's stock. Why shouldn't a firm with a significant short position, say 5 percent or as little as 1 percent, have to disclose its position and identity itself?, the two Wall Street men asked. Cox did not agree.

"I would just like to see the disclosure of this trading," Flaherty said.[12]

"I don't want to penalize people for enterprising and discovering information on their own and using it themselves, and I don't think our law should be designed to prohibit that in any way," Cox said.[13] "I wouldn't think you would either."[14]

Small biotech and publishing companies then testified, saying that they also were victims of false information and rumormongering. The company executives claimed that short sellers had interfered with their businesses to the point where the shorts seemed to be waging an all-out war on their companies. The executives said that short sellers had contacted their bankers, shareholders, suppliers, and customers—along with regulators, journalists, and trade associations—in order to plant false information about the company as well as the personal integrity of the executives, their families, and their friends. The executives said the spreading of these lies was the sole reason for their stocks to crash, not the fundamentals of the companies.

The CEOs complained that the short sales greatly exceeded the number of shares outstanding.

"Let's take an example for you," Cox responded.[15] "You have an annual meeting coming up, annual meeting of shareholders. You set a record date, isn't that right?"[16]

"Yes," said Thomas Marquez, CEO of Carrington Labs.[17]

"Now, at the record date, is it possible through any amount of short selling that the number of record shareholders could be different than your issued and outstanding shares . . . I will tell you, the answer is no. It is not possible," Cox said.[18]

"Let me close with the question that I asked the previous panel, which is why, to the extent that rumors are a problem—and I think that all of us should agree that spreading false rumors is wrong, financially hurtful, ought to be stopped," Cox continued.[19] "Why is it that current laws forbidding such things aren't working?"[20]

"Nobody is enforcing them [the laws]," Marquez said.[21] "Our only choice is to go to court, and you understand . . . the impracticality of going to court."[22]

"Actually, that is something that I think we ought to dwell on," Cox said.[23] He continued at length:

> If the proposal is that the Securities and Exchange Commission police every single instance of malicious rumors about a company anywhere in America, then the taxpayers are quickly going to be funding the SEC at a level which rivals SDI.
>
> It seems to me that we have private enforcement mechanisms. That is the purpose of civil remedies.
>
> My concern is that we not throw the baby out with the bath water. I, for one, believe there are substantial benefits to short selling and, Mr. Marquez, I know that you might at least be of the opinion that short selling ought to be done away with altogether. Some of the proposals that we are considering might have that effect even if it is not intended, and I want to make sure that when we come up with a remedy, it is a remedy targeted at the precise evil. I am also skeptical about the ability of a government agency, even one as efficiently run as the Securities and Exchange Commission and even if we triple its resources, to get at the problem of policing rumors in the market . . . "[24]

Dick Whitney could not have defended short selling any better than Chris Cox did in 1989. But the difference between the hearings of 1932 and 1989 was that this time the government's own agency, the SEC, gave hundreds of pages of testimony that indeed supported the shorts and accepted the short sellers' role as a de facto policing agent for the marketplace. John Struc of the SEC gave his view of Marquez's shorting allegations by presenting a step-by-step analysis of how companies often stretched the truth in order to blame the shorts for their ills. He used Carrington as an example. Their claims of interference by short sellers were not based on fact, he said. Trading volume in the stock did not materially pick up at the times the company said it did. There were also a number of problems with the stock: the FDA had denied approval for a drug the company had in development, the company was thinly capitalized, having only one source of financing, and much of what the shorts had alleged was materially correct.

The SEC said it found five or six factors when it analyzed claims of short manipulation: the agency found that the companies had inadequate disclosure; short selling of the company's stock was a rumor; a significant rise in the stock price was followed by prices falling; the volatility of the stock's price dive was inexplicable; there were technical settlement issues that explained market activity; and there were cases where the shorts got flattened. In other words, there were many reasons to explain shorting activity that were unrelated to bear raids.

Even John Flaherty said that the shorts were right 9 out of 10 times. And the CEOs admitted that the SEC did look at a cross section of these rumors and supposed manipulative activity and found that 27 out of 30 were true—which spelled bad news for the companies. The SEC concluded that a 1-in-10 ratio did not justify the need for law enforcement. If the shorts' research was right 90 percent of the time, and the other 10 percent of the cases of supposed abusive shorting were due to other market factors, then why bother pursuing enforcement actions and investigations?

Some 20 years later, in 2009, the SEC and other regulatory bodies began investigating short selling once again. The arc of how these current investigations proceed will be the same now that the authorities are looking into hedge funds and shorting. The process began in July 2008 when Congress, the White House, and regulators first focused on bear raids, abusive short selling, and rumormongering. This could lead to an investigation into banking practices followed by a lawsuit by the Justice Department, which will try to bring structural reform through litigation.

What is so striking about the Senate and House hearings of the last century is that the roles remain the same. Short sellers are still the bad guys, congressmen are still reacting to the populist will, and chief executives are still saying their companies were victimized by the shorts and asking Congress are and regulators for help, thereby deflecting attention from their own poor management decisions.

Frank Parish, who testified in 1932, is no different from any current CEO who attacks shorting as a cover for his company's own fundamental business problems. Congressional investigations taking place as this book goes to press are similar in nature to commissions led by Pujo, Pecora, or any elected official recognizing a good opportunity for press and the popularity guaranteed from skewering rich people who act like self-styled sovereigns. The speculators who made millions and then billions offer wonderful theater for political sport. This is easy pickings for a media-savvy politician.

Dick Whitney was, in effect, two people—defender of Wall Street and later a convicted crook—and while there are some who represent the former's attributes, there is no sitting leader or spokesperson for the Street canvassing today. Does the absence of a public advocate mean that those who may eventually testify in front of Congress will face ridicule, censure, or jail time? Possibly. What seems nearly certain is that a modern Pecora will investigate the CEOs and market players who enriched themselves while their companies' stock prices and fortunes melted.

The current financial mess has not only savaged personal fortunes and corporate balance sheets, but it has also affected how we interpret the Constitution and the role between the federal government and the financial system. The government's role in regulating Wall Street has had a long and symbiotic relationship with the expansion of federal and executive power. Since the days of Hamilton and Jefferson, Washington and Wall Street have always coexisted in a push-and-pull relationship that allowed them to counterbalance each other, with neither —constitutionally—able to outdo the other. Neither side capitulated.

What makes the events of September 2008 so profoundly unnerving is that one side—Wall Street—was finally outflanked by the other. On September 18, 2008, as the market appeared to be in free fall and the solvency of some of the marquee names in global finance was in doubt, the SEC—the government's financial regulator—gave in to the desires of lobbying Wall Street CEOs looking to protect their equity prices, and banned shorting on financial stocks. Hat in hand, with toxic assets deadening their balance sheets, Wall Street CEOs had to ask for protection from the market forces that they had embraced for so many years. The populist forces that had been waiting to pounce for 230 years had their chance. Any state insurance regulator or credit default swaps trader should probably understand the way banking has gradually become regulated by the federal government.

It is no accident that nearly 60 years after the Pecora Commission—as the animus against supposedly rich, non-tax-paying, freeloading bankers subsided—Wall Street, in 1999, successfully lobbied to be unshackled from the federal constraints of the Glass-Steagall Act, which had restricted a bank's use of depositors' money. Is it any wonder that Wall Street firms felt so omnipotent? They had successfully challenged and won a federal repeal of a federally designed banking system. It took 60 years for the demons of the Great Depression to recede and finally allow Wall Street to combine depositors and risk takers again, with predictably the same results.

But when the tide turned against Wall Street in 2008 and Washington attacked the shorts, regulators unintentionally shut down most of the higher-yielding and essential capital markets, including convertible bonds, a $200 billion market that is often the lender of last resort for companies; high-yield bonds; and distressed debt and equity issuances. Trillions of dollars of liquidity were lost because no one understood how intricately involved shorting was to those markets. The firms that asked for a shorting ban realized that the only way to avoid the same fate as Lehman Brothers, Bear Stearns, and AIG was to tap the last form of liquidity in the market, the buyback mechanism of short selling. This was the same tool Whitney had once relied upon to avert a disaster when the British abandoned the gold standard.

What is particularly galling about the complaints against short selling, and the CEOs' call for regulation, is that many of the flaws in the system were either established or contributed to by the very firms that were appealing for government help. The most vocal firms that blamed the shorts for their woes also, ironically, had the largest prime brokerage businesses—the very businesses that enabled the shorting of almost every stock traded.

The structure of prime brokerage also led to the distortion of short interest (the measure of how much stock is being shorted at any one point in time). Securities cleared offshore and shorted offshore are not required to be reported to the New York Stock Exchange or any other exchange. So we have an absolutely ridiculous situation where financial executives are complaining about the short selling of their own stock. Meanwhile, these same financial executives, through their firms' prime brokerage businesses, make it hard for the management teams of other companies to know the exact size of the short positions being held in their companies' stock. Imagine that. A double standard.

Brokerage executives think, "I was making billions of dollars on products related to short selling and hedge fund clearance. But when it is my stock being shorted, I will get the government to protect me." Government intervention may have saved the financial companies, but this author believes that these companies had no idea that populist sentiment against Wall Street is as deep-seated—or as rooted in history—as it is.

By giving in on the short-selling rule, Wall Street executives have enabled Washington to exercise power over banks and markets in a way the government never dreamed possible. Jefferson's acolytes, now that they have the ability to own and manage banks, will try to reduce corporate influence and power. They will try to increase the power of the federal government and its influence on the economy. Jefferson the populist not only hated the results of speculation; he hated any corporate form that allowed consolidation of financial power. It wasn't just bank power that had Jefferson in a twist, but also the form of corporations.

President Barack Obama is a constitutional scholar who taught constitutional law at the University of Chicago. It won't be lost on him that Wall Street has buried itself. It also won't be lost on him that federal power has expanded through banking issues that had constitutional ramifications. The interpretations of implied powers and the general commerce clause all involved banks. The financial crisis will present President Obama with the opportunity to expand federal or executive power at the expense of corporate authority.

Now the arguments of Hamilton and Jefferson seem to have reversed themselves in ways the founders never intended. President Obama is using Jefferson's populist rhetoric—combined with Hamilton's view that the government should be a centralized force—in order to keep Wall Street under Washington's thumb. Wall Street should study Jefferson and his battle for state sovereignty if it hopes to stop the encroachment of federal authority over capital markets. Wall Street has always wanted a consistent set of rules at the federal level. With Jefferson as its guide, decentralized state regulation might be more attractive.

Whitney's testimony was not only a defense of shorting but also— most important to his constituents—a defense of the New York State–regulated New York Stock Exchange. At Whitney's hearings in the House, much of his testimony dealt with why the Federal Trade Commission should not regulate short selling. He said that federal regulation of shorting would be unconstitutional and a violation of states' rights. Jefferson would agree with Whitney's defense of shorting or Wall Street's resistance today to listing over-the-counter derivatives on a central exchange, but he would be surprised at who is giving the defense.

Was it inevitable that the Jefferson/Hamilton positions would switch sides? It is ironic that Wall Street financial firms, heirs to the imperious Morgan, invited Washington into their houses in the first place. It is even more ironic that the speculators whom Jefferson hated could then actually quote him to get the government back out of their business. But before all of this is over, we are bound to see many more strange happenings.

We can hope that one of these developments is that the populist public actually realizes the shorts aren't the bad guys, never were, and that it was the shorts who provided the honest, good facts that many of the imploding companies never provided themselves. But that may take a bit more history.

EPILOGUE

Richard S. Whitney Before the House Judiciary Committee. The Committee ... Representatives La Guardia, Michener, Tucker, Condon, Celler and ...

WHITNEY DENOUNCES LEGISLATION AIMED AT SHORT SELLING

Practice Is Essential to Maintaining a Stock Market, He Tells House Committee.

KEPT THE EXCHANGE OPEN

Government Regulation Would Mean a Breakdown in Efficiency, He Declares.

TRADING PROVIDES CHECKS

Shorts "Smooth the Waves, but Never Affect the Tides," He Says.

SPECIAL TO THE NEW YORK TIMES.

WASHINGTON, Feb. 24. — Short selling: is essential to the maintenance of stock exchanges, and stock exchanges are necessary to provide a market for investors Richard Whitney, president of the New York Stock Exchange, told House judiciary subcommittee, to day.

... had been no short sellin

WALL ST. DISCUSSES SHORT STOCK SALES

Friends and Foes of Practice Agree a Law Against It Would Curtail Trading Sharply.

BROKERS' PROBLEMS CITED

With Business Reduced, Value of Memberships in Exchange Also Would Shrink.

Agitation in political and oth circles against short selling in th securities markets has directed th attention of brokers to effects whic legislation against that practice would have on the volume of trad ng on the New York Stock Exchange and on the value of memberships in the Exchange.

The supporters and the foes of hort selling agree that any restric ons on that form of trading would sult in a sharp contraction of the siness done on the Exchange. ce the value of memberships ctuates directly with the volume rading, a ban on short selling ld tend to reduce that

e of the making of the contract is the owner or possessor of the curities sold."

The judiciary subcommittee, of ich Representative Tucker of rginia ... listened tentiv ... 12,0 ews. lly uar as c th ve uth nov ar

position because we w could not carry out ou matter of trust."

His summation of th effect of short selling in market, under any conc that this practice "sn ... over affects

short selling wo the activities according to brok ers prefer a mar can buy or sell at

Blow to Tradi Barring of short crease the problem change firms, whose been reduced during years by the decrease tivity and the decli prices. Since their comn with the prices of sec decline of more than 70 the average of stock resulted in a large red these revenues. In Septem more than f

SHORT SELLING OFTE A SUBJECT FOR DEBAT

"Bear" Operators, Censured by Pr dent Hoover, Have Stanch Defend as Well as Sharp Critics

BY EUGENE M. LOKEY.

THE public reaction to Presi dent Hoover's recent censure of "certain gentlemen" "who have been, selling short in the

ably, the short selling cont Meanwhile, certain Sena Representatives in Congre manding legislative restri prevent the dislocation of

To enjoy the advantages of a free market, one must have both buyers and sellers, both bulls and bears. A market without bears would be like a nation without a free press. There would be no one to criticize and restrain the false optimism that always leads to disaster.

—BERNARD BARUCH, FINANCIER,
STATEMENT BEFORE THE COMMITTEE
ON RULES OF THE U.S. HOUSE OF
REPRESENTATIVES, 1917

October 2009 marked the eightieth anniversary of the stock market crash of 1929, which led to a financial and economic wasteland from which the United States and much of the world only emerged after World War II through the institution of the Marshall Plan. The Temporary National Economic Committee of 1937 showed that despite all the fiscal stimuli implemented by the U.S. government to try to jumpstart the economy—namely, the measures introduced in Roosevelt's New Deal—the lingering effect of the Depression remained. These days, it seems impossible to separate our understanding of the Depression and World War II. The war was an elixir to the Depression, and, more significantly, the atrocities of World War II overshadowed the domestic catastrophe inflicted by the trauma of

1929. There were breadlines, unemployment, and starvation, but American domestic life was spared the horrors of fascism.

The Depression occupies a lower ground, as it did then, when viewed from the lofty Churchillian promises that "blood, toil, tears, and sweat" would lead to the "broad, sunlit uplands" of peace, peace in his time. From the high ground of Churchill's rhetoric, the Depression could be seen as less important, less consequential. Its historical wave lapped on the shore and was overcome by a much larger one. It is useful to recall that America has elected a number of presidents who fought in World War II, but no candidate that solely defined himself as a survivor of the Depression has held the highest office in the land. The narrative of Depression-era survival is stirring, but it was not the resonant narrative of a generation. Freedom of movement, expression, and belief—the victory of democracy over tyranny—were more important than any economic ill. Even though we were miserable, so our historical memory tells us, what came after it made the suffering well worthwhile. In hindsight, our basic need to be free was more important than our need to be rich.

Given the recent collapse of the American economy, there are many parallels to the Depression—not all of which are obvious. The similarities could lead to a major reinterpretation of that period of economic history precisely because of the way the credit crisis has transpired. It would seem that the current mess on Wall Street has provincial roots in the Depression. Just as the makers of the economic bubbles of the 1920s were either too old or too young to have fought in World War I, the bankers and executives who presided over this postmillennial mess were either too old or too young to serve in Vietnam (the two wars fought in the Persian Gulf do not apply to the comparison, as we now have a volunteer service). The danger for current Wall Street power brokers is that the Great Crash may be reinterpreted as having been caused not by great economic factors such as Smoot-Hawley or the rise in interest rates, but by a group of counterfeiters and hucksters. It was Wall Street and Wall Street alone that was responsible for the easy leverage of both eras, the purchase of stocks and real estate in the 1920s or, more recently, the boom in real estate and debt-laden leveraged buyouts that enriched the new owners. But we will let history do the redefining and correcting.

Short sellers function as the police officers to markets—the editors—the very checks and balances our forefathers envisioned. The shorts are a disinfectant, shedding light where there is only corporate darkness. In many ways they are the inheritors of the rights of dissent and the rights of minority interests that the founders fought for and designed with such intricate detail. What has happened over the last year is the economic equivalent of Tiananmen Square. I will not argue that the right to short sell is the equivalent of a sole freedom marcher's denying a tank's advance or an Iranian's willingness to give his or her life so that others enjoy the inalienable rights that our founders expressed for the world. But I will say that, in the same way that governments want to discourage dissent and keep their power, corporations have the natural inclination to keep the ranks in file, which has prompted them to engage in a war on shorting.

Controlling the message without a filter is what governments want—it is the central nervous system of any political campaign—and can be an important business strategy for any corporation. When big business becomes so big that it can operate hand in hand with Washington, what is good for business is good for government, and vice versa. In a related sense, what is bad for business is deemed worth using the arms and levers of Washington to police.

The reason that shorting taps into our inalienable rights is that short sellers are financial protesters. Very much like the press, shorts should have the right to ask any question they want. I do not believe that it is a coincidence that a war on shorting coincided with a war on sources for news stories. The press lets out a pretty loud yelp when a reporter goes to jail for protecting sources, preserving the rights defined by the First Amendment. Yet, ironically, the very people who defend the free press—including some of the world's finest journalists and editors at the *New York Times*—also run story after story evidencing a very negative slant against shorts.

In part, short sellers are the *60 Minutes* of the capital markets. They are the investigative reporters who show up at your warehouse and ask if you are dumping toxins into the river, or worse, exporting your bad and mercury-filled computers to China. This is why management hates them so much and wants to do everything it can to get rid of them.

The reason American capital markets are the best in the world is that we have the best information. In many countries, the government is less trustworthy, and there is less capital flow because of the manner in which information is disseminated. Japan is still coping with the fact that it kept altering the number of bad loans the country had in the early 1990s. Every number the Japanese government released was supposed to be final—until the next final number was announced. The government manipulated the information, and now, 15 years later, a significant chunk of the population remains inclined to second-guess the government's official statistics.

By discouraging shorting, this essential transparency—ironically the same transparency that the Obama administration keeps calling for—becomes completely unattainable. In a world where information is incredibly accessible, where it is often a point-and-click or a wiki-site away, there is now a war on accuracy that starts with a war on shorting. We have confused accessibility with accuracy and consequently are making it easier—despite all the public scrutiny on compensation and bonuses—for companies to manipulate earnings, lie about their balance sheets, and distort their overall financial health. It appears we are doing this because the creation of a scapegoat is a successful political tool. But what boggles the mind of any speculator with an understanding of history is that we are repeating a pattern that has never borne prosperity.

During the height of the panic that ensued after the collapse of Lehman Brothers, two things became clear to market participants. First, the firms that were the backbone of the financial system were incredibly interconnected. The idea behind letting Lehman fail was to prove that there was no such thing as being "too big to fail," that regulators and central bankers were determined to show that taking big bets with shareholder money did not end in an exchange of shareholder interests with those of taxpayers. By letting a big firm fail, the regulators figured that they were sending a message that there was no free lunch for Wall Street. They were also saying to the global banks around the world that "we will not bail out your bad bets." Second, the regulators believed that there was enough financial strength in the system to withstand a failure of one major bank.

But the regulators went a step further—they went out and blamed the shorts, restarting what the Senate Banking and Currency Committee put to rest some 80 years earlier. In the immediate aftermath of the failure of Lehman, shorts came under attack from all sorts of people. The attack was global: liberal and conservative politicians, clergyman of all faiths, trade unions, and bank CEOs.

So what did the global regulators and heads of state do in the aftermath of the mortgage debacle? Gordon Brown—a politician in need of an uptick—along with the British Chancellor of the Exchequer, attacked shorting in no uncertain terms at the annual Labour party conference. The British prime minister told the conference that the rights of homeowners come before the rights of a "few hedge funds."

Other European political leaders followed suit. Prime Minister Silvio Berlusconi of Italy called for a ban on "speculative attacks" on Italy's banks. Peer Steinbrück, the German finance minister, piled on as he wanted all "purely speculative short selling" done away with. As events from the 1930s were repeating themselves, the larger economic and difficult regulatory issues were taking a backseat to easy political talking points that could be made by assigning immediate blame to those who could not defend themselves.

Hedge funds and the proprietary trading desks that obtain liquidity by shorting stocks are incredibly press shy because the people who give them money to manage, either investors or the management of the big banks, are hypersensitive to negative press. There is an old adage in the hedge fund industry that says that headline risk is death. This is because the people giving them money provide that capital on a short-term basis, and a transaction that makes controversy is particularly unpalatable.

"I think the hedge funds would have lost the debate anyway, but given that no one turned up, there was no chance of winning the debate," says one of the United Kingdom's largest hedge fund managers, who declined to be named. Dozens of other managers expressed similar sentiments. After the crash, the British press quickly labeled hedge funds "spivs" and "speculators," and few wanted to go public to defend shorting since politicians and regulators were trailing in the media's wake.[1]

Following suit, most of the world's largest stock markets introduced temporary restrictions on short selling—some, like the United States, suspended shorting on 15 percent of the NYSE companies. The number of companies that applied for protection was very high. In the United States, almost 1,000 companies applied to be exempt under the SEC emergency order to ban short sales of financial companies.

But then a funny thing happened. All sorts of firms were calling themselves "financials," even though they had already raised money from the public in all sorts of ways by calling themselves "nonfinancials." Health-care companies, information technology companies, and manufacturers, as well as Ford and IBM, all wanted to be exempt from shorting, alongside insurers and banks. This is why shorting is such an emotional and important issue. Companies need to produce quarterly earnings, and the ways in which they sometimes go about fulfilling that need collides with the investors' right to know the true financial conditions of the companies. But when these truths are exposed by the shorts, a constituency that can easily have points scored against it in the eyes of people who don't fully understand its function, their merits are lost. Perhaps the most poignant maligning of shorting came from England and the archbishops of York and Canterbury, the top Anglican clerics who called on the government to ban short selling and not lose their nerve as "they look to identify more targets." Chaucer, who noted a tradition of corruption in the churches as far back as the fourteenth century, would no doubt have laughed at the irony of the Archbishop of Canterbury calling short sellers "asset strippers and bank robbers."[2]

But some very duplicitous behavior by the critics of shorting came out during the height of the financial crisis. The very critics of shorting by the Church of England were found to have profited from their hedge fund investments—some of whom had shorted stocks as a key point of their strategy. The Liberal Democrats in the United Kingdom were found to have their largest contributor be a hedge fund; members of Parliament had invested in hedge funds as well.

Wall Street CEOs were telling their employees and shareholders that the only thing wrong with their firms was the market's irrational view of them. They believed that fear, rumors, and short selling were reasons that stock prices were falling. Liquidity issues of banks that had borrowed money in the short term only to buy assets in the long term were not addressed. The wholesale funding that supported and then could not support the entire earnings stream of Wall Street firms was being explained by huge numbers that could have quickly disappeared. The amount of credit lines and funding available to the firms was not the same as core capital. Firms knew that the flaw in borrowing short and lending long was exposed, so they did what they always do: they attacked the people they could attack and moved the attention of the debate away from themselves.

What these CEOs also did not realize was that in attacking the shorts and publicly naming them as the main reason for the falling of their stock prices, they were exacerbating their own demise. The hedge funds assets that were held in the prime broker departments of the very same banks having funding problems became nervous that their clients and their own money could find its way into a bankruptcy, resembling what happened at Lehman Brothers Europe. The resultant widening of the credit default spread was caused as much by managers wanting to protect themselves against the failures of the banks that held all their money as anything else.

Wall Street lobbied Washington for a ban and got one. But then a funny thing happened—history repeated itself. Just as it was in 1937 when the SEC introduced an uptick rule, people had forgotten how shorting was so interconnected with the instruments of the capital markets—a mirror image of how institutions were interconnected to one another. After introducing the uptick rule in 1937, regulators started to get complaints that market makers could not do their jobs. They could not provide liquidity at a price, so regulators made consecutive— not concurrent—one-off exceptions. As a result, the SEC gave an exemption to shorting instruments, where the long position was convertible into the underlying stock, like warrant and convertible bonds, and for general market-making activities. Just as it was some 70 years later in 2008, the ban was total at first. There were no "exempted short positions taken as a hedge against holdings of convertible bonds, which can convert into equity. It also allowed shorting by market makers— special traders who match buyers and sellers—and index arbitrageurs, who ensure index futures contracts trade in line with the underlying stocks." Wall Street was powerful enough to shut down the very markets that it would later tap to raise needed capital in the future—such as the preferred stock and convertible bond markets—all because it believed shorting was hurting it. In fact, the ban turned out to be very expensive, as it undoubtedly increased the cost for the capital that needed to be raised in the middle of the crisis.

The regulatory moves effectively put many hedge funds whose sole focus was buying convertible bonds out of business. "The market shut-down was blasted by the industry for destroying the hedge-fund-dominated convertibles market by refusing to exempt hedges against convertible bonds or convertible preferred stock . . . The reason people like us are willing to lend money or invest money in these companies is because we can hedge the underlying risk of the company," fumed the head of one of the largest hedge funds in the United States. "The market is now completely shot as a way for companies to go out and raise capital."[3] In other words, one of the market's best providers of liquidity was being undermined.

The FSA, the U.K. regulator, understood the connectivity of shorting to the rest of the market, but the U.S. regulators did not and only repealed parts of the ban after it became apparent that many other markets—other than the stock market—were dependent on being able to hedge the underlying bonds or preferred stock. But by that time, the ban was on—stocks rose ferociously and caused tremendous losses for the very people that the country needed at that time to lend money (buy bonds) from the very banks who wanted the ban. The buyers, most of them Americans, would have stepped in instead of having foreigners own a substantial part of the banking system. In an odd way we have said that banks are too important to fail, but not important enough that the matter of who owns them is a political or national security issue. To call this a shortsighted strategy is an understatement. No one was thinking of the unintended consequences at the time. There was only the transfer of wealth, from funds and firms that were the victims of the short-sale squeeze on banks to the banks and former investment banks that needed their share prices bolstered.

The ban also effectively identified good versus bad short selling. Short selling that helps companies raise capital is "good." If companies can issue debt in the form of convertible, corporate, preferred stock, or distressed debt, and if the owner wants to hedge the risk of holding the debt by shorting some of the common stock against it, that is morally good. But if someone takes a bet against a company in the form of shorting its common shares, that is morally dubious or "bad." "The Church of England makes this distinction itself in defending its use of currency hedging for its vast investment portfolio, a practice that could be described as shorting entire countries."[4]

Aside from the role shorting plays for companies raising capital, there were further unintended consequences immediately after the ban. The biggest impact was that people could not get their money out of the equity markets as fast or as cheaply as they could before the ban. Liquidity—getting your money when you want it—cost a lot more after the ban. Was that supposed to be the point?

According to Credit Suisse, the cost of trading rose sharply in stocks that can no longer be shorted, as bid-offer spreads—the difference between buying and selling prices at any moment—widened "substantially." The reason was simple: volume plunged as hedge funds stopped taking long positions that they could not hedge with short positions in other stocks.[5]

Analysts at Sandler O'Neill calculated that volumes of trades on U.S. exchanges fell 41 per cent after the ban, with volumes in stocks that can no longer be shorted down 49.6 per cent, while for those that can still be shorted it was down 37.7 per cent. At the same time—as is normal when liquidity dries up—volatility increased sharply, making shares rise or fall faster.

The problem here is that the computer-driven hedge funds that make up 30–40 per cent of trading on the world's major stock exchanges have cut back, as they cannot risk trading without short positions to protect them from overall market movements. The regulators appeared to believe that this was a price worth paying for bolstering financial share prices while the U. S.'s $700 [billion] bail-out plan was put together.[6]

The short-selling ban was instituted because the falling of a bank's stock price—even though it is the most junior piece of paper in the capital structure—was deemed to be the most important piece of financial information in worldwide financial circles. Callum McCarthy, as chairman of the FSA, said that the U.K. watchdog had brought in the ban because it was concerned with "incoherence" in bank shares. He said "movements in equity prices can be translated into uncertainty in the minds of those who place deposits with those institutions with consequent financial stability issues," echoing worries that plunging shares can cause a run on a bank.[7]

The SEC raised the issue of rumormongering by short sellers, where a trader bets against a stock and then spreads false rumors to push down the price. This is already illegal, of course, and it is the nasty rumor that overwhelmingly contributes to the black eye worn by the profession. "This kind of manipulative activity is particularly problematic in the midst of a loss in market confidence," the SEC said. "For example, in the context of a credit crisis where financial institutions face liquidity challenges but are otherwise solvent, a decrease in their share price induced by short selling may lead to further credit tightening for these entities, possibly resulting in loss of confidence in these institutions."[8]

Therein lies the problem that we all face. Short selling is one of the integral forks in the road for how we are going to regulate banking in the future. There have been only a few major reviews of Wall Street by congressional inquiry. I chose to discuss the Pujo and Pecora hearings in earlier chapters because, I think, they more closely resemble the current mood and market circumstances that confront the country. The Brady Commission, though full of many interesting recommendations (one of them was to combine all regulators, something the Obama administration had considered), focused solely on why the crash of 1987 happened, and on very specific trading practices, not on all of Wall Street. The country was willing to give President Ronald Reagan and his team a pass, since most of the country believed that Washington, and not Wall Street, was the cause of economic problems.

In 1907 the Pujo Committee underscored the country's unease with the management of the laissez-faire banking system, which was created by Andrew Jackson's refusal to renew the Second Bank of the United States.[9] The committee took shape to counteract how deeply entrenched Wall Street had become in Washington. The National Monetary Commission was led by a Republican senator from Rhode Island, Nelson Aldrich, who was a good friend of Wall Street, but the recommendations went nowhere because Wall Street understood K Street before there even was a K Street.[10] They "fared well in the Washington arena."[11] So Wall Street was able to schmooze its way out of regulatory harm and scrutiny because it was such a powerful oligopoly.

The Pujo Committee's work was followed by a time in which business was seen as controllable because of the newly perceived relationship between government and big business in the 1920s. With the successful passing of the Clayton Act, which strengthened antitrust regulation, and the establishment of the FTC to enforce the Clayton Act, Stanley Buder, in his *Capitalizing on Change: A Social History of American Business*, contends that the average American finally saw the federal government as an effective "watchdog" on business, and the progressive initiatives "dampened anti–big business sentiment by seemingly offering protection from large corporations."[12]

The FTC was considered the watchdog over capitalism and big corporations. So when the crash happened, Washington's road map was an easy one to regulate Wall Street. The Pecora Commission, recognizing how entrenched Wall Street had become, decided to show the world what some of the guys were up to. It was clear that the opprobrium directed at the bankers was just. The double dealing, insider trading, and manipulation of the stock market were seen for what they were: an insider's game. Matthew Chauncey Brush was asked during his testimony after Whitney to the Senate's Banking and Currency Committee in 1932, "Have they got rackets like Al Capone up there?"

Mr. Brush answered, "Al Capone is a piker compared to that racket."

Brush had replied in a way that captured the power and the criminality that many felt Wall Street had committed.[13] Pecora used the doings of Wall Street to reintroduce proper legislation. I think he brilliantly realized that even though he did not preside over the short-sale hearing, the effect was to soften Wall Street up. The bankers that followed the prominent Wall Street bears were shown up for rigging the game. They were documented under oath, and he skewered them—rightly.

Just as in 1932, the investigations into shorting and rumormongering—still ongoing as of the summer of 2009—are the opening bell. Wall Street complained and got action on something that is very hard to prove: what was the motivation of the seller at the time of sale? Professor Marshall Blume of the Wharton School poses a hypothetical question: "A person has a negative view on the stock; they sell the stock short, and then they call up their friends and say, 'I had a negative view on this stock and sold it short.' And then other people then sell it short;

helping to drive the price down. Is that market manipulation?" What Blume describes is perfectly legal, whereas spreading the same information with the intent to drive the stock price down is illegal. Of course, determining one's intent is a difficult, if not impossible, task.

Wall Street bought some time and deflected the blame of the credit crisis onto short sellers based upon the definition of what the intent was at the time of sale—very tricky ground. If someone did purposely and abusively spread false rumors, the law is pretty clear about what should happen to that person. History has repeatedly demonstrated that there has never been a case of consequence when it comes to proving intent as it pertains to short selling or naked short selling. Something tells me that the Wall Street executives should brush up on Pecora and understand the vitriol that America has historically held for Wall Street.

If there is a litigation of a major player in the money management world who disseminated his belief that the shares of a major financial institution would fall based on his research, then I believe that you have a classic case of First Amendment issues: right to freedom of speech, right to peaceful assembly, right to protest. The case would try to prove that the research was given out with the intent to drive down the shares of the banks and brokers. It will be hard to prove because the numbers are on the side of the shorts. Wall Street firms, despite their protestations to the contrary, were not as well funded as they stated. It is simple: a firm may have had $40 billion in equity capital and $500 billion in debt, but it had over $2 trillion of CDS exposure that it had written to other firms and clients. Once the market thought that the firm could not pay off a significant majority of the $2 trillion in promises to pay what it owed other firms, the core capital of debt and the firm's equity valuations were not near enough to cover its obligations. Every jury will understand that $2 trillion is a bigger number than $500 or so billion—this $2 trillion number would be on top of the souring mortgage, residential, and commercial bonds on the firm's books.

As I already stated, short sellers are financial protesters. As much as the government hates leaks to the media and unexpected front-page stories in the *Washington Post* or *New York Times,* corporations view short sellers as snitches, people who prevent them from controlling the spin on their own companies. Shorts are an interference, or an outright block to the message they want played to the public. If you are the government, it is the CNN watcher, the buyer of newspapers, and the online news browser who get your story. If you are Wall Street, it is the buyers of stocks and bonds. There is one difference, however: politicians do not have to sign a piece of paper that is legally binding to attest to the accuracy of what they say. Corporations do. If they are public, they have to attest to the accuracy of their public statements and filings. It is why we have the best information and best capital markets in the world. What are the suspenders to the belt of possible civil and criminal litigation? Short selling.

At the very beginning of the credit crisis, I was fascinated by how the crisis quickly morphed into a Main Street versus Wall Street argument. Did Wall Street cause the panic? Wasn't it those greedy bankers who caused all these problems? No one in the media bothered to try to explain how the fracas between Wall Street and Main Street reached its boiling point. This is one of the reasons that I decided to write this book.

All my friends on Wall Street said that it was a ridiculous argument. Main Street is Wall Street; they are the same; there is no difference. They were completely—even as smart as some of them are—unaware of the anger that was brewing in the country over the paychecks and self-appointed entitlement—"my business is more important than your business, so I need government money more than you do"—mentality. There was just this very strange feeling that the credit crisis had actually revealed that some of the most basic assumptions we had made about one another were wrong. Wall Street felt that since it runs the most important businesses in town—after all, what is more important than credit—we were all in this together.

Main Street felt differently, "Small business, 'the little fellow,' occupies a special niche in the pantheon of national heroes. Small business is regarded as quintessentially American. To many Americans, the large corporation remains an intimidating and impersonal abstraction. In contrast, small business is identified with familiar faces—the small-town shopkeeper, the insurance broker whom you can call with personal problems. Small business is assumed to have stronger loyalty and ties. But above all, small business symbolizes the persistent American ideals of the self-made man or woman, opportunities for social mobility, and perhaps as important, the Jeffersonian theme of independence gained by being one's own boss. It is in some ways the 'last American frontier.'"[14] The Main Streeters had felt that their idea of a modern frontier, of figuring out a way to be their own bosses and carve out a place where they could pursue their own dreams, was distinctly American. They felt it was an ideal under threat by men in business suits on the southern tip of a small island.

In this crisis, my appreciation for American history and for the founding of this country was renewed. For all the stories, books, articles, and blogs that I read while researching this book, I was fascinated that not one of them actually addressed the issue of why Main Street feels the way it does about Wall Street. I had a hunch that there was something in the nation's founding that could explain not only why we feel the way we do but also how our feelings take on different vehicles over time. There are very real historical antecedents that show we are doing nothing but repeating what our founding fathers did so many years ago.

APPENDIX

New York Times Articles

VOTE WIDE INQUIRY ON SHORT SELLING

Senators, Without Debate, Authorize a Sweeping Investigation by Banking Committee.

"BEAR RAID" IS DESCRIBED

Pipe Line Head Accuses Stand and Oil and Doherty Concern of Causing "Disaster."

SPECIAL TO THE NEW YORK TIMES.

WASHINGTON, March 4. — The Senate, as forecast, brushed aside its customary routine today to rush adoption of a resolution authorizing a "wide open" investigation of stock exchanges by the Senate Committee on Banking and Currency.

The resolution, introduced late yesterday on behalf of that committee, was adopted without debate after being reported favorably by the Committee on Audit and Control. By unanimous consent the Senate waived the rule requiring that such reported resolutions lie over for one day, as this would have involved a, delay until Monday.

The Banking and Currency Committee immediately made plans to meet on Tuesday, when it will determine procedure, consider what witnesses will be called first and select the experts to guide its investigation. The resolution carried an appropriation of $50,000 for these expenses.

Just before this action was taken, a House Judiciary subcommittee received testimony detailing an alleged "bear raid" on the stock of the Missouri-Kansas Pipe Line Company on June 16, 1930, which caused the stock, listed on the New York Curb, to drop from an opening of 36¼ to 15.

Frank P. Parish, president of the company, charged in a statement submitted for him by Representative Gregory, of Kentucky, that the break in the stock occurred after he had refused to accede to demands made by the Standard Oil Company of New Jersey and H. L. Doherty & Co. He said that an order to buy 100,000 shares of the stock was insufficient to sustain the market.

Mr. Parish's, statement, which was admitted to the House subcommittee record without public reading, said that L. E. Fischer, vice president of the North American Light and Power Company, had warned him of the attack on the pipe line stock.

Mr. Parish said that during this visit, on June 14, Mr. Fischer was accompanied by W. G. Maguire, a broker. He stated that he asked Mr. Fischer to arrange a meeting between himself and Christy Payne, vice president of the Standard Oil Company of New Jersey.

Mr. Parish said that Mr. Fischer offered a truce for one week, but that when he arrived in New York on June 16, the attack on the stock had begun.

"We were not able to see Mr. Payne on the day of the raid until 4 o'clock in the afternoon," Mr. Parish said. "On entering his office we found Mr. R. Carr with him. Mr. Carr, I understand, is president and counsel for Columbia Carbon Company. Mr. McGuire was also present.

"Immediately after introductions, Mr. Payne smilingly asked: 'How do you like it?'

"I said: 'How do I like the market of Missouri-Kansas?' He just grinned and I replied that it was 'not too bad.'"

Describing the alleged raid, he went on:

"Mr. Fischer said that unless I would abandon the Missouri-Kansas Pipe Line Company project and cause that company to sell all of its gas reserves to the Standard Oil of New Jersey, and all of our pipe lines and pipe contracts to H. L. Dohertv & Co., the market on Missouri-Kansas Pipe Line Company stock would be attacked and raided on June 16; that I would be bankrupt and thoroughly discredited, and that if I showed opposition I would even be attacked personally and slandered and my family attacked; that I would not be capable of bucking such powerful interests as Standard Oil of New Jersey and Doherty."

Effects of Raid "Disastrous."

"As an inducement to accept the proposal, Mr. Fischer said that he was authorized to offer my company a 15 percent interest in the common stock of the Northern States Pipe Line Company (then under construction toward Omaha and the Twin Cities) at cost," Mr. Parish said. "I replied that I could not possibly accept such a proposal and endeavored in my conversation to avoid an open break."

Mr. Parish related other conferences which, he said, were without results, and added that the alleged attack occurred as scheduled on June 16 when "all my supporting bids, approximately 100,000 shares at 36⅛ to 36¼, were filled before I could possibly withdraw them."

Effects of the break have been "disastrous to this day," Mr. Parish added, "for not only has the company suffered a financial loss, mounting into the millions of dollars, thereby, but our 21,000 shareholders in forty-six States have likewise been innocent victims.

"Their confidence in our ability and integrity has been impaired or virtually destroyed, the available markets for natural gas have been shut off from Missouri-Kansas Pipe Line Company and practically every source of credit has been closed.

"To rescue our enterprise from total collapse." Mr. Parish continued, "the Missouri-Kansas Pipe Line Company was forced in September, 1930, to dispose of a 50 percent interest in the $40,000,000 natural gas pipe line system, then under construction from Texas to Indiana, known as the Panhandle Eastern Pipe Line Company; it has been compelled to halt the investment of additional capital in the development of its natural gas reserves in Western Kansas and in pipe lines in that State and in Indiana."

Mr. Parish added that "certain conspirators have themselves embarked upon a policy of 'rule or ruin,' and short selling has been but one of their weapons in clubbing those who stand in their way."

$50,000 for Senate Inquiry.

Passage of the Senate resolution authorizing a wide market investigation constituted the final step in preparation for the inquiry. An appropriation of $50,000 was included.

"What effect do you think this investigation will have on the stock market?" Chairman Norbeck was asked.

"I don't know, and I don't care," he replied.

Asked again about a list of witnesses which Senator Walcott was reported to have said the committee possessed. Senator Norbeck replied with equal emphasis: "There are no witnesses yet."

Senator Walcott, whose suggestion I of an inquiry into short selling, made after a conference with President Hoover, resulted in the committee's decision to make a comprehensive investigation, said he hoped that the hearings may be terminated soon. He added, however, that he would not attempt to control them.

As market declines have been more predominant than security-value increases for more than two years, first attention probably will be paid to allegations that impetus was given to the declines by short sellers, or so-called "bear raiders."

Payne Denies "Raid" Charge.

Christy Payne, a director of the Standard Oil Company of New Jersey, in charge of the company's natural gas interests, yesterday described as false the charges made by Mr. Parish.

"I met Mr. Parish only once in my life, and had no business dealings with him," Mr. Payne said. "I have taken no interest of any kind, nor has my company, in the affairs of the Missouri-Kansas Pipe Line Company. Neither I nor anybody acting for our company, or our company, has ever bought or sold a share of stock of the Missouri-Kansas Pipe Line Company.

"The charge that we sold short the shares of that company is preposterous. In fact, we have had no relations of any character with that company and have not taken any steps to influence or interfere with its development and operations.

"There is not the slightest ground for the charges in so far as they relate to this company or to me as an individual."

The Missouri-Kansas Pipe Line Company brought suit for $75,000,000 Feb. 14 against Henry L. Doherty & Co., Henry L. Doherty, Standard Oil Company of New Jersey, and the North American Light & Power Company.

The suit charged a conspiracy to "break" the Missouri-Kansas Company by blocking its financing plans.

BEARS PLANNED RAID, SENATORS WERE TOLD

Group With $1,000,000,000 Reported to Have Prepared Coup for Yesterday.

WHITNEY IS IN WASHINGTON

La Guardia, in House, Asserts Brokers Threatened a Panic if Inquiry Was Started.

SPECIAL TO THE NEW YORK TIMES.

WASHINGTON, April 9.—The Senate stock market investigation starting Monday has the approval of President Hoover, Senator Walcott stated today.

"The President is in full accord with what we have done and is absolutely back of us," the Senator said.

This announcement was construed as refuting reports that the decision to begin the investigation, taken suddenly yesterday afternoon by the Banking and Currency Committee, was made by radical Senators who took advantage of the absence of Senator Norbeck, chairman of the committee.

In connection with the Senator's statement it was recalled that he had originally proposed the investigation in February immediately after a conference with the President.

Two reasons were ascribed today for the sudden decision to start the inquiry, dormant up to yesterday, at once. One was that some Senators had been informed that a gigantic bear raid, backed by $1,000,000,000, was to be made today. The other was that some Senators had been told that bear raiders and certain foreign interests were responsible for declines in the market this week that set new low records for some of the leading stocks.

These reports apparently had been heard by all those concerned with the investigation, but no one would admit knowledge of their origin.

La Guardia Charges Threat.

In the face of these rumors was the fact that the stock market moved upward today. This was interpreted here as meaning either that the decision to start the investigation had averted a bear raid, if one was planned, or driven the short interests to cover, increased buying causing a normal rise in prices.

The rise of the market also came at a time when Representative La Guardia of New York declared on the floor of the House that unnamed brokers had threatened to create a panic if the market was investigated.

Richard Whitney, president of the New York Stock Exchange, summoned to testify under oath before the Banking and Currency Committee when it opens its investigation Monday, was here today, but declined to discuss the inquiry on the ground that courtesy to the Senators forbade comment by him until he goes on the witness stand.

In discussing market .conditions, however, he stated that "wash sales," or false transactions, were virtually non-existent. There had been only an infinitesimal number of such sales in the last ten years, and each violation has been followed by the imposition of severe corrective measures by the Exchange.

Mr. Whitney was called before the House Judiciary Committee early this year, and in his testimony, covering virtually every phase of stock market operations, insisted that short sales were essential to the maintenance of an open market.

No Plans Beyond Monday.

The present inquiry, however, will go beyond that conducted by the House committee. The Senate committee has requested definite information concerning: short sales and the names of those making them. A sergeant-at-arms of the Senate was in New York today assembling records desired by the committee.

Other developments indicated that the investigation may not go beyond the taking of Mr. Whitney's testimony, unless the committee gathers information Monday which will form a basis for further study. It is generally understood that no other witnesses have been called. One influential member of the committee privately termed the investigation "humbug."

The action of the committee in determining to push the investigation, although announced as having been reached unanimously, was taken in the absence not only of Senator Norbeck but also of Senator Glass. The latter would make no comment on the action, but he announced that the banking bill, of which he is the author, now before a subcommittee of which he is chairman, was virtually ready to be reported to the full committee and that he planned to present it Monday afternoon. Such procedure may interfere with the inquiry, since the committee has voted to give this bill precedence.

There was doubt today as to whether the committee's action relative to the inquiry overruled the previous decision but Senator Glass said:

"The stock market investigation will not interfere with my bill if I have the authority to prevent it—and I think I have that authority."

Three for Extended Inquiry.

One Senator told newspaper men that a large number of telegrams had been received asking for the stock market investigation and that one of these had come from George Carr Baker, publicity manager of the Republican National Committee in 1924 and active in the 1928 campaign for President Hoover.

Three Senators on the committee apparently will press for an extended inquiry. These were named by Senator Brookhart as himself and Senators Couzens and Blaine.

"If they try to use this for a political bludgeon," Senator Brookhart said, "they will have myself, Couzens and Blaine to reckon with. This investigation is like a snowball and we shall keep it rolling."

He touched on the rumors of "wash sales," saying one broker had told him that "nine-tenths of the sales on the stock market today are wash sales."

Further light was shed on what occurred at the informal meeting in the Republican cloakroom when the decision to open the inquiry was made. Senator Walcott, according to various versions, called the committee members together, although Senator Brookhart was the ranking member in the absence of Senator Norbeck, Senator Walcott talked with Mr. Whitney, who was in New York, on the telephone and was informed by the latter that he did not feel free as an officer of the Stock Exchange voluntarily to make public the facts requested. Accordingly, the members decided to issue a subpoena, which Mr. Whitney said he would accept. Senator Brookhart, on another telephone, listened in on the conversation.

Senators Walcott and Steiwer drew up the subpoena, calling for the production ot facts concerning short sales as of April 8. This was said to have been an inadvertence, as the committee actually wanted the records of April 7.

All this was learned by Senator Norbeck this morning and he heard it apparently with considerable surprise.

The Senate having adjourned until Monday, few Senators were at the Capitol today, but there was curiosity as to what the reaction will be when the body reconvenes and finds that an investigation is being conducted exclusively into the practice of short-selling.

The Senate, a month ago, opposed what was termed a "one-sided investigation." Senator Walcott's proposal for an inquiry into short selling aroused a storm of objections and the protestants demanded that if any Investigation were made it should cover all ends.

Accordingly, the Banking and Currency Committee drew up a resolution under which the Senate would instruct it to conduct a wide-open investigation of buying and selling and of the borrowing and lending of securities on stock markets. This was passed with an appropriation of 550,000.

BEAR RAID INQUIRY OPENS

Whitney Holds Public Is 'Trying to Give This Country Away.'

SCOFFS AT TALES OF PLOT

Senators Told '120,000,000 Bulls' of 1929 Were Real Cause of Slump.

BOOM-TIME POLITICS CITED

Short Selling Accounts for Only 5 Per Cent of Stock Trading, He Testifies.

SPECIAL TO THE NEW YORK TIMES.

WASHINGTON, April 11.— Richard Whitney, president of the New York Stock Exchange, testifying today before the Senate Banking and Currency Committee, flatly denied that bear raids take place on the Stock Exchange.

Mr. Whitney cited figures showing that during two recent severe declines in the market the short interests actually operated in decreasing amounts of stock as the market declined, rather than larger amounts.

Had there been the semblance of a raid, he said—and he contended this would have been impossible under the surveillance imposed by the Exchange on all transactions— the short sales would have increased as the market declined.

Shrinkage in Short Position.

On April 1, when the House passed the tax bill, adversely affecting the market, the short position totaled 3,279,000 shares, Mr. Whitney testified. The market fell off sharply in succeeding days, but on April 6 the short position had dropped by 220,000 shares to 3,059,000.

"Then the market dropped in spite of short covering?" asked Senator Bulkley.

"Yes," replied Mr. Whitney. "I can't see the argument that short interests caused the decline."

Mr. Whitney also cited the bear market between Sept. 11 and Oct. 9, 1931, when stocks dropped precipitately, but during which time, he said, the short interest declined by 2,200,000 shares.

Blames Liquidation Movement.

Other outstanding points in Mr. Whitney's testimony were:

1. That liquidation of securities by their owners is exerting a far more depressing effect on the market than any other cause.

2. That short-selling has generally accounted, since the depression began, for less than 5 per cent of all Stock Exchange transactions.

3. That prohibition of short-selling would close the stock markets and freeze the security for bank loans of between $5,000,000,000 and $6,000,000,000.

4. That the deflation, in part, represents a state of fear in which "many people are trying to give this country of ours away."

5. That the speculative mania cul-

minating in the crash of 1929 originated in the education of the public to invest in securities during the sale of Liberty bonds.

While not so testifying directly, Mr. Whitney agreed with statements by Senator Morrison of North Carolina, that the depression was intensified by efforts on the part of administration leaders to sustain the market in 1929 with statements of confidence. Ha said the actual depression began in March of 1929.

Defers Naming the Shorts.

At the opening of his testimony, Mr. Whitney promised to produce the names of large short operators and the stocks affected by their operations, as requested in the committee's subpoena, but said this might be deferred until Friday, as the information must be compiled by 175 experts working over reports from 25,000 brokerage offices in the United States.

The testimony of Mr. Whitney, which will be continued tomorrow, ranged from financial dissertations to pointed political observations. Occasionally there was laughter, as when Mr. Whitney met Senator Brookhart on the latter's own ground and illustrated a broad financial reference by using a figurative cow to make clear his point.

The committee room, designed to accommodate about fifty spectators, in addition to newspaper men, held close to 500. A curious group stood so close behind Mr. Whitney's chair and those of the Senators that they leaned with their elbows on the backs of the chairs.

Whitney Holds His Audience.

Long rows of spectators sat on filing cases around the walls, and the less fortunate stood in their places for hours to hear the highest authority on the Stock Exchange explain its intricacies. The testimony was sufficiently interesting to hold the audience throughout the day.

Occasionally there was a roar of laughter, as when Senator Glass leaned forward, following Senator Morrison's questioning of Mr. Whitney concerning what was termed the false impetus given to the market from political quarters, and pointedly referred to a Republican campaign slogan of 1928, saying: "You are referring to a chicken in every pot?"

"We did not mention it, Senator, but we had it in mind," responded Senator Morrison.

The committee held an executive session lasting almost an hour after the hearing, but arrived at no decision as to future witnesses. Senator Glass's banking bill will be taken up after the questioning of Mr. Whitney has been concluded, it was decided.

The committee took under advisement the question of scaling down the amount of data requested from the Stock Exchange.

No action was taken on a demand by Senator Blaine that a telegram from George Barr Baker, active in the Hoover campaign of 1928, and one of those suggesting the stock market investigation, be made public.

The investigation was begun by Senator Walcott immediately after a conference with President Hoover Feb. 26. The Senator announced last Saturday that it had the endorsement of the President.

Explains That Task Is a Big One.

At the start of his testimony Mr. Whitney read a detailed explanation of the vast amount of work required to give the committee a list of all corporations in which there was a short account of 10,000 or more shares at the close of business April 8, and a list of customers short 200 or more shares. He promised, however, that it would be provided.

The witness was advised occasionally by his counsel, Roland L. Redmond. The committee counsel, who questioned Mr. Whitney on some details, was Claude R. Branch of Providence, R.I. Mr. Whitney put into the record detailed reports of many phases of trading previously made public. Mr. Branch brought out that no record has been made of short sales covered on the same day made. These will be compiled for the committee.

Mr. Whitney said the Exchange had issued public statements of short-selling operations covering the period since March 25, 1931, "because we desired to put fully before the minds of the people of the entire country the facts that existed with regard to short selling and in order, as we saw it. to prove that the exaggerations with regard to it were absolutely ridiculous."

Unaware of Great Bear Raid.

Senator Brookhart recalled the hurried conference of some members of the committee last Friday in the Senate Republican cloakroom, when it was decided to call Mr. Whitney.

"It was represented to this committee," said Mr. Brookhart, "that there was a list, or a combination rather, of big bear dealers who were selling on Friday last a large quantity of stocks short, and that they had planned to make a Black Friday out of Saturday, and that you had the names or knew who they were, but refused to disclose that information. Can you tell us about that?"

"I had no knowledge, Senator, of any bear raid," replied Mr. Whitney, "beyond what was conveyed to me over the telephone with particular regard to United States Steel by Senator Walcott. And I have no knowledge now of any bear raid.

"Our investigation, made as a result of the request of Senator Walcott into the operations of our specific stocks, United States Steel, American Telephone and Telegraph. Public Service of New Jersey and Consolidated Gas of New York, showed no bear raiding, but did show great liquidation for long account."

The witness defined a bear raid as "an illegitimate attempt to demoralize the market," punished severely by the Stock Exchange and almost impossible of accomplishment. He said such raids might be attempted without short selling and that the same demoralization could occur in an unchecked bull market.

As to the Public and Mistakes.

Senator Gore sought to bring out that short selling and marginal dealing in securities are parallel transactions, buyer and seller each gambling on his judgment in hope of a profit, with one invariably being wrong. Senator Glass observed dryly:

"It is astounding to learn that there have been any mistakes."

These mistakes were made by the "people of the United States, not only by brokers," the witness suggested.

"Then, Mr. Whitney," interposed Senator Blaine, "you refer to those whom Mr. Hoover described in 1912 as the idiots who come in and get stocks after they have been pushed up to almost unknown heights—the public—do you not?"

"I have no knowledge of and have ever seen any statement made by the President with regard to that," was the reply.

"Then you ought to go over to the Congressional Library and the The London Mining Journal, I believe, of May, 1912," Senator Blaine said. "It might be very useful to the New York Stock Exchange."

"I do not doubt it." replied Mr. Whitney, his smile fixed, "but we have a great many other things to do at this time."

In response to Senator Couzens, the witness stated that he did not know of investment trusts lending stocks to short sellers.

Asks Witness to Play Bear Raider.

Senator Brookhart suddenly asked: "Will you give us an illustration of how a bear raid can be conducted? Run one for us a little while and let us see what it is like."

"I never have," said Mr. Whitney, crinkling his brow in bewilderment. "You know how fellows run them that do run them, don't you?"

"No, sir."

Under further questioning the witness explained the theoretical procedure of selling stocks "as quickly as possible and in as demoralizing a way as possible." He explained later that this practice was checked by a rule preventing a short sale at a price less than the last previous quotation of the stocks involved.

Senator Brookhart referred back to the investment trust question, particularly regarding United Corporation, which drew the dry comment from Mr. Whitney that "I own some of its stock and my children do, which was bought at prices averaging around 50. It now sells at about 5."

Senator Brookhart recalled the questioning of Mr. Whitney by Rep-resentative La Guardia of New York when the Stock Exchange official testified before the House Judiciary Committee in January. Mr. La Guardia then declared that the stock of United once sold at a total figure greater than the value of the stock held in trust, and that it had dropped from a valuation of $1,400,-000,000 in 1929 to about $175,000,000.

Mr. Whitney replied that he "did not put the stock up, and did not put it down." He disclaimed knowledge of the figures cited by Senator Brookhart, but added that he understood "the facts stated by Mr. La Guardia do not agree with the facts."

Brookhart Calls 1929 a "Bull Raid."

Senator Brookhart asked if the appreciation of stocks in 1929 was not due to a "bull raid."

"Indulged in by 120,000,000 of people of the United States, yes," was the reply.

Q.—Led by the New York Stock Exchange? A.—I deny that. sir.

Q.—It does not lead anything? A.—It is a market place.

Q.—It takes their money and lets them go? A.—The New York Stock Exchange does not take anybody's money.

Q.— Well, the members do; it is all the same thing? A.—They are paid for executing of orders, just as you are paid for being a real estate broker or a banker, or whatever It may be.

Senator Glass inquired if Mr. Whitney thought the public had "any idea of the intrinsic value of stocks in which they were investing, to use a polite term?"

The reply was a citation of the numerous statistical services available to investors.

The hearing eventually returned to the central purpose—an investigation of short-selling. Mr. Whitney pointed out that every short sale must be completed through actual payment for and delivery of stock. Senator Glass inquired closely into this point, but Mr. Whitney stuck to his contention, saying that otherwise the transaction would be bucket-shopping, which is prohibited by law.

Points to the War Financing.

Senators Blaine and Brookhart pressed the questioning on the splitting of shares, "wash sales" and so on, but the witness countered with the statement that inflation was caused only by the investing public, trained to investment in securities by war-financing publicity.

"Before the war there was a billion dollars of debt of the United States Government," he said, "and they sold approximately $20,000,000,000 of bonds to the people of this country, and therefore engendered in those people a knowledge of securities which they have maintained to this day—an interest in securities."

He told Senator Brookhart that corporations received more money from the beginning of 1929 until the stock market break than the total increase in brokers' loans in that period, indicating that investing and not speculation accounted for the majority of the sales of securities. He conceded that much stock buying is "gambling," but said both kinds of buying are necessary to maintain a liquid market.

"You think, then, that a liquid market is advantageous, even though it is being constantly depressed?" asked Senator Steiwer.

"I think it is vital," replied Mr. Whitney. "We have some five or six billions of loans held by our banks throughout this country on collateral security listed on the New York Stock Exchange. If the Stock Exchange did not have a liquid market, if that market were closed, as would in my opinion happen by the prohibition of short selling, those five or six billions of collateral loans would be frozen, and the gravity of our banking situation I do not think can be overestimated."

Says the Pendulum Swung Too Far.

"There is no market now, is there?" asked Senator Glass.

"There is a tremendous market now, yes, sir," was the reply.

"Did not prices reach a place where they exceeded any business-like estimate of the value of the stocks based on earnings?" Senator Morrison asked.

"Yes, sir, the pendulum swung too far that way," Mr. Whitney answered.

Q.—The charge has been made that the brokers were doing that and leading the thought of the country to make money out of it; but the influence of other people who have the attention and the confidence of the public boosting things could contribute as much as anything the brokers said, could it not? A.—Unquestionably.

Q.—If the President of the United States should in such a situation make the boosting statements, the Secretary of the Treasury make the boosting statements, and other great leaders of public thought, it would tend to carry that thing on, would it not, just as much as some broker saying it? A.—Yes, sir.

Q.—About that time the whole country had about reached the state of mind that they thought poverty was about to be abolished in our country forever, had they not? A.— Yes, sir. A new era was with us.

Q.—And great public men were leading the country to think along that line, were they not?

A.—Yes, sir.

Q.—And the whole public thought the days of hard times and anything like poverty had passed away forever, and the high-powered salesman was being tremendously aided by the high-powered political agent of prosperity was he not? A.—Yes. sir.

Senator Glass here interjected his remark about the "chicken in the pot," and the committee adjourned for luncheon amid laughter.

Member's Firm Disciplined.

During the recess Senators learned that leading issues in the market were setting new low records. Mr. Whitney conferred by telephone with Stock Exchange officials in New York City, and when the committee reconvened he said:

"The business conduct committee [of the Exchange] has reported on all sales of 500 shares or more, and we find that there are no bear raids, practically no short sales and that practically all sales were for liquidating long accounts. I have just been in communication with the chairman of that committee regarding today's reports, and he says the situation is the same, with great liquidation going on." Under questioning by Mr. Branch, Mr. Whitney said that less than two weeks ago a questionable transaction that had the appearance of a bear raid on American Telephone and Telegraph stock was discovered in a transaction made through a member brokerage firm—a short sale below the last quoted price.

He said the Exchange member of the firm was not disciplined, as he did not know of the transaction, but that "we immediately declared this firm an undesirable partnership and the partnership was dissolved." He said another such instance occurred several months ago.

The business conduct committee of the Exchange, he testified, has made "two, three, possibly five, thousand investigations of suspicious transactions," there being twenty trained accountants "continually going into brokerage offices on cases referred to the committee."

Senator Blaine, a wet, remarked to Senator Brookhart that "evidently Exchange rules are enforced better than prohibition agents handle your law."

Mr. Whitney, in response to a question by Senator Gore, said that "a long sale is really more depressing to the market than a short sale."

"The short seller," he testified, "has to go into the market to buy again, but the party long on stock, who sells, need never buy or sell again if he does not wish to do so."

Between May 25 and Nov. 30, 1931, the witness testified, "less than 5 per cent of all transactions were for short accounts, more than 95 per cent were for long accounts, and I have no reason to believe that the general percentage rate has changed."

"Mr. Whitney," remarked Senator Glass, "I am beginning to wonder what you are here for, anyway."

The witness shook his head.

"Was there any unusual short selling last Friday?" asked Senator Bulkley.

"There was not," replied Mr. Whitney.

"Then I am wondering what you are doing down here?" asked Senator Glass again. "Whence came those reports of an organized bear raid?"

"I really do not know," said Mr. Whitney. The spectators laughed. "Nothing we could find proved a bear raid had taken place."

Glass Recalls High Tariff.

The witness, speaking as a practical farmer, endeavored to illustrate to Senator Brookhart the fact that no blame could be placed on any group of individuals for the depression, by comparing it to the purchase of a cow, for a "good round sum" which might die of an unexpected disease a short while later.

When Senator Brookhart asked Mr. Whitney if present conditions in the security market create any advantage for agriculture, Senator Glass interposed:

"No, and you won't see any advantage either, for when the next election comes along you will vote for the same old protective tariff."

(Senator Brookhart will run on the Republican ticket in Iowa for re-election this Fall.)

Mr. Whitney showed to the committee members a chart on which was depicted the stock price trend during the last seven months, together with notations of important national or world events. Stocks advanced, the chart showed, when the Reconstruction Finance Corporation act was passed; they reacted favorably to the passage of the Glass-Steagall bank relief bill, and they fell off when the House passed the lax bill; but generally there were no great upturns or downward trends.

Senator Glass examined the chart, and then remarked:

"To show how mythical are these fluctuations, as for instance the so-called Glass-Steagall bill, I'll ask you how many applications have been made for loans under that bill."

"I don't know," confessed Mr. Whitney.

"Then I'll tell you," said Senator Glass. "Just one!"

In closing his testimony for the day, Mr. Whitney said that last week the market was "dreadful."

"To what do you attribute that?" asked Senator Bulkley.

"To liquidation mostly," replied Mr. Whitney. "There also were large withdrawals of gold from the country; statements of corporation earnings were lower; the presentation by an accounting firm that Kreuger & Toll's figures had been falsified, possibly as far back as 1924; and, if I may say it, the proposed taxes have created great concern among the investors in this country."

MARKET RESUMES DECLINE.

Persistent Liquidation Carries Prices to New Low Levels.

With President Richard Whitney of the New York Stock Exchange submitting in Washington to an extended interrogation on short selling by a Senate committee, the share market resumed its decline yesterday on a broad front under the pressure of persistent liquidation.

Stocks broke sharply in the early dealings, carrying the price averages to levels that had not previously been touched in possibly eighteen or twenty years. In some instances, quotations fell almost to the prices prevailing after the depression of 1907.

There was a fairly smart rally in the last hour of trading, with the result that some of the earlier losses were canceled. However, net declines were wide in many sections of the list, ranging from 1 to 6 points or more in prominent issues.

The combined averages of The New York Times showed a net loss of $2.39 on the day. Twenty-five industrials were off an average of $3.72 and twenty-five rails fell $1.05. The total turnover on the Stock Exchange was about 1,700,000 shares.

Among the stocks which bore the brunt of the selling were Auburn Auto, which ended 3% points lower on the day; Santa Fe, an exceptionally weak issue, which closed 7% points down; American Can, off 2%; American Tobacco, off 8 in slow trading; Drug. Inc., off 3%; du Pont 6 per cent debentures, 6; Detroit Edison, 4; United States Steel, 1%; Union Pacific, 5; National Biscuit, 2%; General Motors, 1/2, and American Telephone, 2.

The weakness was ascribed by brokers mainly to liquidation, which, in their opinion, was induced by the uncertainties with respect to tax legislation and to the disappointed hope of an early Spring revival in trade and industry.

Short selling contributed to the un-settlement, no doubt, but speculative operations on the down side were conducted cautiously. Traders already short of the market were said to be less anxious after the announcement that the inquiry into short selling would not, for the present, extend beyond the questioning of Mr. Whitney and the presentation of the information which the Senate committee asked him to produce.

The clerical forces of the Stock Exchange and its subsidiary, the Stock Clearing Corporation, continued yesterday the compilation of the data required. Disappointment was fell in Wall Street that full information on the subject could not be presented at the first hearing.

The impression in the financial community is that the investigation will produce no sensations and that it will not uncover evidence of bear raid plots or of unusual activities by shorts. Brokers and their customers were generally pleased by the testimony of Mr. Whitney and their judgment, according to the brokers' circulars, was that he had acquitted himself favorably.

The bond market participated in yesterday's downturn. All sections were under pressure, including United States Government obligations which have been uniformly strong for some time. Domestic corporation and foreign issues were sold in considerable volume on the Stock Exchange.

st of Shorts on the Stock Exchange on April 8 as Given Out by the Senate

CALLED IN SENATE SHORT-SELLING INQUIRY.

Percy A. Rockefeller, Nephew of John D. Rockefeller.

Matthew C. Brush, President of American International Corp.

GLOSSARY

Assumption. The plan put forth by Alexander Hamilton to solidify government finances by consolidating state IOUs, state debt, and federal debt under the credit standing of the newly formed government of the United States.

Balance Sheet. 1. A balance sheet is the compilation of what a company owns and owes. 2. Balance sheets are something most hedge fund managers don't think they have as their bankers have convinced them that the amount of fees coming from their fund to the management company has a true multiple to it and makes them a cashless business.

Bear Raid. The opposite of a short squeeze—a group of short sellers colluding and shorting a company's stock at the same time. During the 1930s, many of the stock-operating pools would collect money from one another and put the capital together to either artificially pump the stock up and let it crash or short a targeted company.

Bear Sale. An antiquated term that means that long sellers, rather than a short sale, are actually the reason for a stock's decline.

Cash Market. Any place where securities are bought and sold for cash and where prices are quoted in dollar terms, not in interest rates. The place where transactions are made to fund the buying and selling of securities is called the financing markets, and they are quoted in interest rates.

Clearing. Clearing refers to how financial firms settle payments between one another for themselves and for their customers

Collateral. Stocks, bonds, or cash pledged to the account of an institution to borrow securities or money.

Convertible Bond. A bond that contains an option in it.

Credit Default Swaps (CDS). A non–balance sheet item and a way of hedging exposure on a bond or an expected payment from a counterparty. The seller of a swap is guaranteeing the creditworthiness of the instrument sold. The buyer is paying for protection on the underlying name. It helps if the hedge is executed with a firm that stays in business.

Free Cash. The difference between margin paid and margin collected.

Gross Exposure. The sum total of long positions plus short positions.

Haircut. In a securities loan transaction, a haircut is the amount of collateral that is needed to exceed the market value of the securities lent. For example, if a bank lends a security that has a market value of $100 and receives $105 from the borrower, the extra $5 would mean that there was a 5 percent haircut, or overcollateralization on the transaction.

In a situation where the borrower is borrowing money, a 5 percent haircut would mean that on $100 worth of collateral, the borrower would receive a loan of $95.

Leverage (also known as "Gearing"). Perhaps the least understood word on Wall Street. In short, leverage is the borrowing of money in excess of your capital. When people on the Street say "I am leveraged 2:1," they mean they have borrowed $2 for every $1 of capital they have.

But leverage can have multiple definitions. Some say it is the amount of long positions divided by capital. Others say it is the amount of long and short positions added together. The number in excess of 100 is said to be levered. For example, if I have $100,000,000 in capital and have $70,000,000 that I have bought, but also have $70,000,000 that I have shorted, the sum total $140,000,000 is my gross, or $40,000,000 over my capital of $100,000,000—so I am levered to the tune of $40,000,000.

Liquidity. The lifeblood of any market. Liquidity represents the willingness of market participants to commit capital so that buyers and sellers can get their money when they want it.

Locate. When a short seller wants to short a stock, he must borrow it first so that he can short it and make delivery to the buyer. The process of identifying the location of the firm that has the stock in inventory to lend is called a locate.

Margin. The amount of money needed to be pledged to a bank in order to buy a security. For example, when putting up 20 cents and borrowing 80 cents to buy a security worth a dollar, the 20 cents is the margin requirement and the 80 cents the lent amount.

"Naked" Short Selling. Corporate chieftains' favorite whipping boy for their failed strategies. Naked shorting is the selling of shares that have not been borrowed. Critics contend that hedge funds purposely do not borrow shares (right away this discredits them) while selling them through their brokers. What they claim is that by not borrowing the stock, which involves selling securities that have not been borrowed, that the seller has willfully distorted the amount of lendable shares that can be borrowed. The naked shorter has created shares to short that are in excess of what is on the books and record of the issuing company.

Net Exposure. Long positions minus short positions.

Prime Brokers. The part of any bank that actually borrows and lends stock and money to investment managers. Also, the area of the bank that gives permission to customers to borrow stock so that they can short it. The prime broker has to give permission to its customers to borrow.

A prime broker actually is many different things wrapped into one. It started out as a banking business to lend money to people—hedge funds and money managers—that traditional banks stayed away from. In performing this function, prime brokers had to provide many services:

- They provided custody for assets.
- They held and collected all the assets of the customer.
- They cleared and settled trades.
- They became the back office for the hedge fund clients, as the hedge fund had no operations to keep track of all the trades it did because it would buy and sell through many firms.
- They became the operating system for the entire hedge fund industry. By providing income statement reporting to their hedge fund and money manager clients, prime brokers became the bankers to the entire hedge fund world.

Repo Market. The marketplace where the bank's balance sheet is turned into leverage and money. The repo market is where banks finance their purchases and sales of items that are on their balance sheets. It is the marketplace where large banks interact with central banks and the wholesale funding market where firms finance themselves.

Rubinstein, Sergei. The life of Sergei Rubinstein is one of the least documented and most intriguing financial stories of the postwar years. *Time* described his life as "a rococo embroidery of lies, boasts, swindles, treacheries, beautiful women and rich living." He was, like Richard Whitney, deeply entrenched in the upper-crust societies of New York, Washington, and various international centers of wealth. New York society columns followed his every move, one describing his 1941 White House reception by President Roosevelt on the eve of his wedding to a celebrated model.[1] Despite his ongoing legal trouble (the *Times* characterized his career as a "20-year duel with [the] law"), Rubinstein always seemed to get away, using his personal fortune and social connections to wiggle out of close encounters. While in New York, he maintained a five-story townhouse on Fifth Avenue replete with tessellated marble floors, carved paneling, a distinguished art collection, and a staircase so grand that in the opinion of one reporter it belonged in a stage set, not a home.[2]

Although the society pages loved his consistent extravagance and the "swarms of women" he attracted, most of Rubinstein's coverage was in the financial press, which labeled Rubinstein the business "sensation of four continents."[3] Part of his mystique drew from his origins. Born in Czarist St. Petersburg in 1909, Rubinstein soon fled with his family to Sweden, his coats allegedly stuffed with money and jewels. His father had been a confidant of Rasputin's, but after the Bolsheviks took over, the family suffered financially and he was on his own. After graduating from Cambridge, Rubinstein rose up the ranks in a French bank and then the Chosen Corporation, where he made millions managing Chinese government bonds and operating three gold mines in Korea.[4] In 1935, France deported him on account of suspicious financial activity, but Rubenstein claimed the premier was simply upset with him for "dallying with his mistress, a French marquise."[5] In 1938, he entered the United States on a fake Portuguese passport he purchased in Shanghai for $2,000, and his career on Wall Street took off. By 1941, Rubinstein had received his first major charge for looting $5.9 million from the Chosen Corporation, beginning a string of illegal activities that would eventually revolve around short selling.[6]

The government did manage to nail him once, in 1949, for dodging the draft for the fifteenth time, but after serving two years in the federal penitentiary, Rubinstein was back on Wall Street, as big a player as ever. The largest and most publicized case brought against Rubinstein occurred in 1951. Court documents stated the government's case as follows:

> Rubinstein ran up the price of Panhandle stock by creating an atmosphere of "big deals" that had no basis in fact and by circulating false and misleading statements . . . that Rubinstein advanced $420,000 — later recovered — so that Panhandle could buy James Stewart & Company, an old established construction company that was virtually bankrupt at that time . . . [and] when Panhandle stock reached a level fourteen times what it had been before the Rubenstein era, Rubinstein sold out, adding $78,000 to his profits by selling the stock short . . . through a dummy, a British business man imported for the purpose.[7]

The scheme was virtually identical to the great pools of the 1920s, but the pools were now entirely illegal. Even so, and perhaps in part because of his stellar legal defense from Connecticut senator Brien McMahon, he was acquitted the following year. Would Rubinstein have been acquitted in Pecora's court two decades earlier, with a record on par with Richard Whitney? The leniency granted to Rubinstein seems indicative of a change in the national mood.

In the end, like Whitney, Rubinstein received his comeuppance. On January 28, 1955, was found by his butler, bound, gagged, and choked to death in his bedroom, wearing his very own custom silk pajamas.[8]

Time magazine wrote, "Agatha Christie could not have thought of a better opening scene," and joked the police had "narrowed the list of suspects down to 10,000."[9] Although some directors disagree, Rubinstein's compelling life story was undoubtedly the inspiration for the 1956 blockbuster *Death of a Scoundrel*.[10]

To this day, the case is open and unsolved.[11] Thus, while the country moved beyond the scapegoating of the Depression era, short selling, on occasion, was associated with the crooks, and in extremely memorable ways.

Second Derivative of the Credit Crisis. The credit crisis preceded short selling or any "attack" on our financial system. Simply put, financial institutions were insolvent. Their generic capital structure of $40 billion in equity market capitalization and $500 billion in issued debt could not support the system of payments that they had created in their mortgage areas and credit default swaps businesses. The math is simple: if half of the assets that a bank would hold in inventory are worth half as much, can that bank make good on all the payments it promises to make through the credit default swaps that it has issued off its balance sheet? And how much does the leverage ratio of the bank go up when the inventory it holds is worth half as much? Unlike the securities held on its balance sheet, short selling did not cause this problem. The funding—the amount of temporary borrowing—that firms could do at the time would have been swamped by their CDS exposure.

Second Derivative of Prime Brokerage. Just as the second derivative of the credit crisis revealed that all the models in the world by all the smartest people could not contemplate the nonperformance by an entity that was supposed to guarantee or limit exposure to subprime, balance sheet is what makes prime brokerage such a fantastic business. Money managers and their investors are unaware of the exposure they have created by engaging a prime broker. The prime broker happily performs the portfolio reporting and other back-office services to be in the position to take custody of the assets that a hedge fund manager has. The manager has no idea that there is a second derivative to all the stock bought and sold—the financing market. The interest cost, allocated by the prime broker, is totally blind to him.

Settlement. Ensuring that what is bought or sold actually ends up in the right accounts, in the right—and accurate—sizes and values.

Short Selling. Shorting a stock is not the opposite of buying a stock. In a short-sale transaction, the entity that wants to sell must first call its executing broker or prime broker to see whether the stock can be borrowed. Once this entity figures out how much stock is available to borrow, it then can execute the sale of the security. The short sale involves a commission paid for the sale of the stock. The short seller must also pay a daily interest fee for borrowing the stock from the prime broker. The interest rate charges can be very high.

Since the numbers of shares that are issued are finite for every issuing company, it is logical that the more shares that are shorted, the higher the interest rate cost of the borrow. Since not every holder of stock has to lend—holders have the right not to lend if they wish—the supply/demand dynamics can eat into the profit of any trade, and in some cases make the entire trade a loser based on the borrow cost.

There is also capital and collateral cost in a short sale. In order to have a prime broker borrow stock for the client, the client must collateralize the prime broker, with cash or securities. The client must also give the prime broker anywhere from 105 to 150 percent of collateral. So if one shorts a stock worth $100,000,000, the prime broker would negotiate to put up either $5,000,000 or $50,000,000 in excess of the $100,000,000. The short seller may not receive interest on the excess—the amount above $100,000,000, in this case $5,000,000 or $50,000,000—further adding to the cost of the transaction.

The aim of a short sale is to profit, after all the costs, from the falling price of a stock. If in our example we shorted 1,000,000 shares of a $100 stock, and the stock fell to $90, we would make 10 points, or 10 points times 1,000,000 shares, or $10,000,000 minus the cost of borrowing those shares, collateralizing the prime broker, and paying the dividend to the buyer.

Short Selling and Financial Terrorism. I had many reasonable, veteran, senior professionals call me up during the week that preceded the Lehman bankruptcy to expound theories that terrorists were taking down our financial institutions in the same way that firms were affected by 9/11. The sequence of how firms were failing was seen to match the attacks on Wall Street that very sunny and clear September day. Such was the level and the intensity of the feeling on Wall Street at the time.

It was interesting to me that Wall Street had not only come up with a very weird explanation, but had also succeeded in comparing its new enemy, short sellers, with Osama Bin Laden.

Short Squeeze. Opposite of a bear raid, a short squeeze is when mutual fund managers, who tend to be long only, size up the short seller as the least capitalized player at the poker table. A short seller has unlimited risk, as the stock can go up as high as the market wants to take it, but he has limited upside, because the most he can make is if the market falls to zero. If a stock is at $70, the most he can make is $70 per share.

If the trade being executed gets crowded, either because it has many other people who are short in it or because the cost of the stock borrow gets too high or tight, many large institutions will purposely buy that stock to force the seller to buy as well and cover or "flatten" his position. Generally the firms that are short are not as well capitalized and don't have the staying power that the large "long only" players do. This lack of capital causes the short seller to scramble to cover the shorts in order to lessen losses and thereby make the shares go even higher.

Stock Loan or Securities Lending Business. This is one of the largest OTC trading markets in the world. This business is what makes short selling possible. In a securities lending transaction, the holder of a security will lend his stock to another party who wants to sell it. In a typical transaction, an agent bank—one that is the custodian for large institutional money managers, pension funds, endowments, and foundations—will lend the securities of its clients to the prime brokerage departments of broker dealers. The prime brokerage departments in turn lend to other broker dealers, money managers, and hedge funds that want to short stock. The agent bank will lend the clients' stock and get collateral to secure any market or credit exposure that it may have.

For example, if an agent bank lent a security that had a market value of $100, it may ask for $105 back in collateral. Most important, the lender of securities is compensated in rent for the loan he engages in. Each security has an interest rate that the lender can charge the borrower. The rate can change in seconds, but is not published anywhere.

The market for securities lending is highly stratified where the pension funds that hold securities usually only want their securities lent to creditworthy counterparts (who is to say what that is today)—namely banks and broker dealers—even though they receive cash or cash equivalents as securities. Once a broker dealer gets his hands on the securities he wishes to borrow, he will then turn around and lend the same securities just borrowed from the banks to a hedge fund. Because the hedge fund is perceived to be a lesser credit than the broker dealer, there is a big rate difference, or spread, between what the broker dealer borrowed the securities for and what he lends them for. Unlike fixed income securities, this market has no floor, or maximum interest rate that the borrower can pay. In the recent meltdown, the shares of Citigroup traded as high as 100 percent fee on a per annum basis. At 100 percent, you can see why the market has resisted calls for transparency and fairness.

Uptick. A rule established by the SEC in 1934 and mandated in 1938. By having trades that are short executed at a price that is higher than the price of the last trade, the uptick rule was a way to try to dampen the momentum of a stock that was being heavily shorted. The uptick rule was fairly effective when bid-ask spreads were wider; the plethora of financial instruments available today make replicating a short strategy easier in other products, such as options.

Weighting. The percent that each position takes in your portfolio. In a $100 portfolio, a $5 position has a 5 percent weighting.

Notes

Preface

1. Charles Jones, "The SEC Brings Back the 1930s," *Columbia Business School Public Offering*, July 18, 2008, www4.gsb.columbia.edu/ publicoffering/post/139305/The+SEC+Brings+Back+the+1930s.

2. John Toland, *The Rising Sun: The Decline and Fall of the Japanese Empire, 1936–1945* (New York: Modern Library, 2008).

Acknowledgments

1. "Norman Mailer Interview," *Academy of Achievement*, June 14, 2004, www.achievement.org/autodoc/page/Mai0int-1.

Chapter 1

1. Jonathan R. Macey, Mark Mitchell, and Jeffrey Netter, "Restrictions on Short Sales: An Analysis of the Uptick Rule and Its Role in View of the 1987 Stock Market Crash," *Cornell Law Review*, 74.5, July 1989, 802, www. heinonline.org/HOL/Page?collection=journals&handle= hein.journals/clqv74&id=951.

2. U.S. Congress House of Representatives, 101st Congress, First Session, Hearings Before the Commerce, Consumer, and Monetary Affairs Subcommittee (introduced in the U.S. Senate; Nov. 28, 1989), viewed Apr. 2009 LexisNexis, New York Public Library Science, Industry, and Business, 16.

3. James Edward Meeker, *The Work of the Stock Exchange* (New York: The Ronald Press, 1922), 96.

4. "Milestones in Short-Selling History," *Reuters*, July 16, 2008.

5. Meeker, *The Work of the Stock Exchange*, 96.

6. Ibid., 97.

7. Kara Scannell and Jenny Strasburg, "SEC Moves to Curb Short-Selling," *Wall Street Journal*, July 16, 2008.

8. *New York Times*, July 19, 1931.

9. Frank Partnoy, *Infectious Greed* (New York: Henry Holt, 2003), 209.

10. Ibid., 209–210.

11. Ron Chernow, *Alexander Hamilton* (New York: Penguin Group, 2005), 298.

12. Ibid., 299.

13. Ibid., 313.

14. Ibid.

15. Ibid., 314.

16. Ibid., 357.

17. Ibid., 359.

18. Ibid., 346.

19. Ibid.

20. Ibid.

21. Ibid., 347.

22. Ibid., 356.

Chapter 2

1. Steve Fraser, *Wall Street: America's Dream Palace* (Hartford, CT: Yale University Press, 2008), 22.

2. "Frederick Jackson Turner," *Encyclopedia Britannica*, May 4, 2009, www.britannica.com/EBchecked/topic/610263/Frederick-Jackson-Turner.

3. Lacy K. Ford Jr., "Frontier Democracy: The Turner Thesis Revisited," *Journal of the Early Republic*, 13.2, Summer 1993, 4.

4. William Appleman Williams, "The Frontier Thesis and American Foreign Policy," *The Pacific Historical Review*, 24.4, Nov. 1955, 380.

5. Frederick Jackson Turner, *The Frontier in American History* (New York: Henry Holt, 1935), www.xroads.virginia.edu/~HYPER/TURNER/ home.html.

6. Williams, "The Frontier Thesis," 381–382.

7. Ibid.

Chapter 3

1. Ron Chernow, *The House of Morgan* (New York: Simon & Schuster, 1990), 149.

2. Fraser, *Wall Street: America's Dream Palace*, 43–44.

3. Vincent P. Carosso, "The Wall Street Money Trust from Pujo through Medina," *Business History Review* (Harvard), 427.

4. "Baker Admits Peril to Nation in Bank Control; Surprises Pujo Committee by Saying Money Concentration Has Gone about Far Enough," *New York Times*, Jan. 11, 1913.

5. "Say Money Trust Is Not Disclosed," *New York Times*, Dec. 1, 1913.

6. Doris Kearns Goodwin, *The Fitzgeralds and the Kennedys: An American Saga* (New York: Simon & Schuster, 1987), 235.

7. Carosso, "The Wall Street Money Trust," 422.

8. "Pujo's Men Besiege Wm. Rockefeller," *New York Times*, Dec. 31, 1912.

9. "Find Rockefeller Too Ill to Answer," *New York Times*, Feb. 8, 1913.

10. Testimony of J. P. Morgan on the Money Trust Investigation to the Subcommittee of the Committee on Banking and Currency, U.S. House of Representatives, courtesy of Securities and Exchange Commission Historical Society, www.sechistorical.org.

11. Ibid.

12. "Money Monopoly an Impossibility, Morgan Asserts," *New York Times*, Dec. 20, 1920.

13. Carosso, "The Wall Street Money Trust," 428.

14. David Kennedy, *Freedom from Fear: The American People in Depression and War, 1929-1945* (New York: Oxford University Press, 1999), 17.

15. Ibid.

16. Ibid.

17. Carosso, "The Wall Street Money Trust," 425.

Chapter 4

1. Justice Litle, *The Roaring Twenties Began with a Commodities Bust*, Nov. 5, 2008, Taipan Publishing Group, Apr. 30, 2009, www.taipan publishinggroup.com/Taipan-Daily-110508.html.

2. Justice Litle, *Why Today's Crisis Is More Like 1919 Than 1930*, 2007–2008, www.straightstocks.com.

3. Litle, *The Roaring Twenties*.

4. Ibid.

5. Ibid.

6. Litle, *Why Today's Crisis*.

7. Ibid.

8. John Kenneth Galbraith, *The Great Crash: 1929* (New York: Houghton Mifflin Company, 1997), 169.

9. Chernow, *The House of Morgan*, 303.

10. "Stock Exchange Itself to Establish Rates to Be Paid for Borrowing of Securities," *New York Times*, June 28, 1931.

11. Chernow, *The House of Morgan*, 307.

12. "Money Monopoly an Impossibility, Morgan Asserts," *New York Times*.

13. Ibid.

14. Ibid.

15. Ibid.

16. Ibid.

17. Chernow, *The House of Morgan*, 351.

18. Ibid.

19. Murray N. Rothbard, *America's Great Depression*, fifth ed. (Auburn: The Ludwig von Mises Institute, 2000), Apr. 14, 2009, www.mises.org/rothbard/agd.pdf.

20. Chernow, *The House of Morgan*, 352.

Chapter 5

1. "Bears Planned Raid, Senators Were Told," *New York Times*, Apr. 10, 1932.

2. "Vote Wide Inquiry on Short Selling," *New York Times*, Mar. 5, 1932.

3. Ibid.

4. Ibid.

5. Ibid.

6. Ibid.

7. Ibid.

8. "Triumph in Gas," *Time*, Feb. 10, 1936, www.time.com/time/ magazine/article/0,9171,755829-2,00.html.

9. "Gas Man's Trial," *Time*, May 13, 1935, www.time.com/time/ magazine/article/0,9171,754773-2,00.html.

10. Ibid.

11. Ibid.

12. "Practice of Short Selling Again Attacked as Unethical," *New York Times*, Oct. 4, 1931.

13. Ibid.

14. Ibid.

15. Ibid.

16. "Wall St. Discusses Short Stock Sales," *New York Times*, Oct. 4, 1931.

17. Ibid.

18. "Whitney Declares Short Sales Vital," *New York Times*, Oct. 17, 1931.

19. Ibid.

20. Ibid.

21. Ibid.

Chapter 6

1. "Whitney Denounces Legislation Aimed at Short Selling," *New York Times*, Feb. 25, 1932.

2. Ibid.

3. Ibid.

4. Ibid.

5. Ibid.

6. Ibid.

7. Ibid.

8. Ibid.

9. Ibid.

10. Ibid.

11. Ibid.

12. Ibid.

13. Ibid.

14. Ibid.

15. "Wall Street Inquiry by Senate Monday; Whitney Summoned," *New York Times*, Apr. 9, 1932.

16. Ibid.

17. Ibid.

18. "Bears Planned Raid, Senators Were Told," *New York Times*.

19. Ibid.

20. Ibid.

21. "Bear Raid Inquiry Opens," *New York Times*, Apr. 12, 1932.

22. Ibid.

23. Ibid.

24. Ibid.

25. Ibid.

26. "Whitney Testifies 2-Week Drop Cost Market 6 Billions," *New York Times*, Apr. 13, 1932.

27. Ibid.

28. Ibid.

29. "Whitney Denounces Legislation Aimed at Short Selling," *New York Times*.

30. "Bear Raid Inquiry Opens," *New York Times*.

31. "Whitney Denounces Legislation Aimed at Short Selling," *New York Times*.

32. "Wall St. Discusses Short Stock Sales," *New York Times*.

33. Ibid.

34. "Practice of Short Selling Again Attacked as Unethical," *New York Times*.

35. "Porcupine Quartet," *Time*, Feb. 27, 1933, www.time.com/time/magazine/article/0,9171,745223,00.html.

36. "Bear Hunt Cont'd," *Time*, May 2, 1932, www.time.com/time/magazine/article/0,9171,743713-1,00.html.

37. Ibid.

38. "NYT on Short Selling," *New York Times*, Oct. 18, 1930, www.bigpicture.typepad.com/comments/2008/09/short-selling-o.html.

39. Fraser, *Wall Street: America's Dream Palace*, 34.

40. "Ex-Knight," *Time*, Mar. 21, 1938, www.time.com/time/magazine/article/0,9171,788235-1,00.html.

41. Ibid.

Chapter 7

1. Amanda Smith, *Hostage to Fortune: The Letters of Joseph P. Kennedy* (New York: Viking, 2001), 112.

2. James Bianco cited in *Wall Street Journal,* July 2008.

Chapter 8

1. "Bear Raid Inquiry Opens," *New York Times.*

2. "Favor Untermyer for Stock Inquiry," *New York Times,* Apr. 4, 1932.

3. Chernow, *The House of Morgan,* 370.

4. Ferdinand Pecora, *Wall Street Under Oath: The Story of Our Modern Money Changers* (New York: Simon & Schuster, 1939), 28.

5. Chernow, *The House of Morgan,* 371.

6. Ibid., 372.

7. Ibid., 370.

8. Pecora, *Wall Street Under Oath,* 37.

9. Ibid., 79.

10. Ibid., 79.

11. Chernow, *The House of Morgan,* 356.

12. Pecora, *Wall Street Under Oath,* 161.

13. Franklin Delano Roosevelt, "Only Thing We Have to Fear Is Fear Itself," First Inaugural Address, 1933, www.historymatters.gmu.edu/d/5057/.

14. Franklin Delano Roosevelt, "Commonwealth Club Address," 1932, www.americanrhetoric.com/speeches/fdrcommonwealth.htm.

15. Charles M. Jones, "Shorting Restrictions, Liquidity, and Returns," Graduate School of Business, Columbia University and NYSE, June 2003, 11, www.wpweb2.tepper.cmu.edu/wfa/wfapdf/shortliq3.pdf.

16. Ibid., 18.

17. Ibid., 17.

18. Ibid., 19.

19. Ibid., 1.

20. Ibid., 8.

21. Ibid., 7.

22. Robert A. Brady, "Reports and Conclusions of the Temporary National Economic Committee," *The Economic Journal*, 53.212, Dec. 1943, 411.

23. Ralph F. De Bedts, "The First Chairmen of the Securities and Exchange Commission: Successful Ambassadors of the New Deal to Wall Street," *American Journal of Economics and Sociology*, 23.2, Apr. 1964, 165.

24. Mike Brewster, "Joseph Kennedy's Enduring Example," *BusinessWeek*, May 29, 2003.

25. Ted Schwarz, *Joseph P. Kennedy: The Mogul, the Mob, the Statesman, and the Making of an American Myth* (New York: John Wiley & Sons, 2003), 107–108.

26. Brewster, "Joseph Kennedy's Enduring Example."

27. Ibid.

28. "The Twilight of TNEC," *Time*, Apr. 14, 1941.

29. David Kennedy, *Freedom from Fear*, 354.

30. "The Twilight of TNEC," *Time*.

31. Kennedy, *Freedom from Fear*, 353.

32. Ibid., 354.

Chapter 9

1. Charles R. Geisst, *Monopolies in America: Empire Builders & Their Enemies from Jay Gould to Bill Gates* (New York: Oxford University Press, 2000), 199.

2. Chernow, *The House of Morgan*, 502.

3. Ibid.

4. Geisst, *Monopolies in America*.

5. Chernow, *The House of Morgan*, 503.

6. Ibid.

7. Ibid., 505.

8. Geisst, *Monopolies in America*, 201.

9. Chernow, *The House of Morgan*, 506.

10. Vincent P. Carosso, "Washington and Wall Street: The New Deal and Investment Bankers, 1933–1940," *President and Fellows of Harvard College: The Business History Review*, 435.

11. Chernow, *The House of Morgan*, 505.

Chapter 10

1. U.S. Congress, House of Representatives, 101st Congress, First Session, Hearings Before the Commerce, Consumer, and Monetary Affairs Subcommittee (introduced in the U.S. Senate; Nov. 28, 1989), viewed Apr. 2009 LexisNexis, New York Public Library Science, Industry, and Business, 87-88.

2. Ibid., 84.

3. Ibid.

4. Ibid.

5. Ibid.

6. Ibid.

7. Ibid.

8. Ibid.

9. Ibid.

10. Ibid.

11. Ibid., 84–85.

12. Ibid., 85.

13. Ibid.

14. Ibid.

15. Ibid., 165.

16. Ibid.

17. Ibid.

18. Ibid., 165–166.

19. Ibid., 167.

20. Ibid.

21. Ibid.

22. Ibid.

23. Ibid.

24. Ibid., 170.

Epilogue

1. James Mackintosh, "Short Shrift," *Financial Times*, Oct. 4, 2008.

2. Ibid.

3. Ibid.

4. Ibid.

5. Ibid.

6. Ibid.

7. Ibid.

8. Ibid.

9. Stanley Buder, *Capitalizing on Change: A Social History of American Business* (Chapel Hill: University of North Carolina Press, 2009), 215.

10. Ibid., 216.

11. Ibid., 228.

12. Ibid., 231.

13. "Bear Hunt Cont'd," *Time*, 1930.

14. Buder, *Capitalizing on Change*, 418.

Glossary

1. "The Scoundrel," *Time*, Feb. 7, 1955.

2. "Death Ends Huge-Stake, 20-Year Duel with Law," *New York Times*, Jan. 28, 1955.

3. "Rubinstein Trial for Fraud Opens," *New York Times*, Jan. 26, 1951.

4. "Death Ends Huge-Stake," *New York Times*.

5. "The Scoundrel," *Time*.

6. "Death Ends Huge-Stake," *New York Times*.

7. "Rubinstein Trial," *New York Times*.

8. "Rubinstein Found Strangled in His Fifth Ave. Mansion," *New York Times*, Jan. 28, 1955.

9. "The Scoundrel," *Time*.

10. "'Death of a Scoundrel' at Loew's State," *New York Times*, Nov. 6, 1956.

11. "Follow-Up on the News," *New York Times*, June 20, 1976.

REFERENCES

Aljalian, Natasha N., "Fourteenth Amendment Personhood: Fact or Fiction?" *St. John's Law Review*, Spring 1999, www.howstuff works.com/framed.htm?parent=corporation-person.htm&url= http://findarticles.com/p/articles/mi_qa3735/is_199904/ai_n88363 70/print.

America's Great Depression, fifth edition, ed. Murray N. Rothbard, (Auburn: The Ludwig von Mises Institute, 2000), Apr. 14, 2009.

Anand, Vineeta, "Short Sale IRS Rule Due in '94," *Crain Communications*, Mar. 21, 1994, www.lexisnexis.com/us/lnacademic/results/ docview/docview.do?docLinkInd=true&risb=21_T4162886285&f ormat=GNBFI&sort=RELEVANCE&startDocNo=1&resultsUrl Key=29_T4162886219&cisb=22_T4162886218&treeMax=true& treeWidth=0&csi=8094&docNo=12.

Anderson, Jenny, "S.E.C. Unveils Measures to Limit Short-Selling," *New York Times*, July 16, 2008, www.nytimes.com/2008/07/16/ business/16short.html?ref=business.

_____, "Wall Street Shudders After Hedge Fund Ruling," *International Herald Tribune*, Feb. 24, 2007, www.lexisnexis.com/us/lnacademic/ results/docview/docview.do?docLinkInd=true&risb=21_T426127 9353&format=GNBFI&sort=RELEVANCE&startDocNo=76&r esultsUrlKey=29_T4261279356&cisb=22_T4262276641&treeM ax=true&treeWidth=0&csi=8357&docNo=82.

Antonio, Antonios, and Ian Garrett, "To What Extent Did Stock Index Futures Contribute to the October 1987 Stock Market Crash?" *The Economic Journal*, vol. 103, no. 421, Nov. 1993, 1444-61, www.jstor.org/sici?sici=00130133(199311)103%3A421%3C1444%3ATWEDSI%3E2.0.CO%3B2-A.

Armitstead, Louise, and Helen Power, "Hedge Funds in Turmoil," *The Sunday Telegraph*, July 13, 2008.

Avery, Helen, "Hedge Funds and Prime Brokers: A Rocky Patch in a Marriage of Convenience," *Euromoney*, Nov. 2007.

_____, "Hedge Fund Holdings Reach Highs," *Euromoney*, May 2008.

_____, "Prime Brokerage Costs Up but Who Cares?" *Euromoney*, Feb. 2008, www.lexisnexis.com/us/lnacademic/results/docview/docview.do?docLinkInd=true&risb=21_T4262089108&format=GNBFI&sort=RELEVANCE&startDocNo=1&resultsUrlKey=29_T4261279356&cisb=22_T4261279355&treeMax=true&treeWidth=0&csi=318063&docNo=10.

_____, "Prime Brokers; Managers Lament Shortcomings of Capital Intro," *Euromoney*, Sept. 2006, www.lexisnexis.com/us/lnacademic/results/docview/docview.do?docLinkInd=true&risb=21_T4261279353&format=GNBFI&sort=RELEVANCE&startDocNo=1&resultsUrlKey=29_T4261279356&cisb=22_T4261279355&treeMax=true&treeWidth=0&csi=318063&docNo=9.

Baer, Justin, "Comeback Chiefs Return to Stage a Second Act; Executives on Wall Street Have a Better Chance of Rebounding from Career Setbacks Than Their Counterparts in Other Industries," *Financial Times*, Mar. 27, 2008, www.proquest.umi.com/pqdweb?index=13&did=1452581341&SrchMode=1&sid=2&Fmt=3&VInst=PROD&VType=PQD&RQT=309&VName=PQD&TS=1217595364&clientId=12498.

"Baker Admits to Peril to Nation in Bank Control; Surprises Pujo Committee by Saying Money Concentration Has Gone About Far Enough," *New York Times*, Jan. 11, 1913.

Barber, Brad M., and Terrance Odean, "The Internet and the Investor," *The Journal of Economic Perspectives*, 15.1, Winter 2001,www.jstor .org/sici?sici=0895-3309(200124)15:1%3C41:TIATI%3E2.0.CO;2-1.

Barr, Alistair, "SEC to Limit Shorting of Fannie, Freddie, Brokers: Emergency Order Will Try to Protect Struggling Firms Against 'Naked Shorting,'" *Marketwatch*, July 15, 2008, www.marketwatch .com/news/story/sec-limit-shorting-fannie-freddie/story .aspx?guid=%7B2B08DEE5-8D5F-47D6-A2D4-7DD5E CEE0D5B%7D.

Bartley, Robert L., "1929 and All That," *Wall Street Journal*, Nov. 24, 1987, page 1, *Proquest*, New York Public Library Science, Industry & Business, www.proquest.umi.com/pqdweb?index=2&did= 27321036&SrchMode=2&sid=2&Fmt=3&VInst=PROD&VTyp e=PQD&RQT=309&VName=PQD&TS=1215798167&clientId =12498.

Bary, Andrew, "Black Monday," *Barron's*, Oct. 15 2007, www.proquest .umi.com/pqdweb?index=5&did=1367177111&SrchMode=1&si d=1&Fmt=3&VInst=PROD&VType=PQD&RQT=309&VNam e=PQD&TS=1217528465&clientId=12498.

"Bear Hunt," *Time*, Apr. 25, 1932, www.time.com/time/magazine/ article/0,9171,743645-1,00.html.

"Bear Hunt (cont'd)," *Time*, 2 May 2, 1932, www.time.com/time/ magazine/article/0,9171,753295,00.html.

"Bear Raid Inquiry Opens," *New York Times*, Apr. 12, 1932.

"Bears Planned Raid Senators Were Told," *New York Times*, Apr. 19, 1932.

Behrmann, Neil, "More Hedge Funds in UK, Europe Expected to Close; Freeze on Investor Withdrawals Sounds Death Knell; Banks Checking Credit Lines," *The Business Times Singapore*, Mar. 22, 2008.

Berkeley, Alfred, "NASDAQ's Technology Floor: Its President Takes Stock," *IEEE Spectrum*, Feb. 1997.

Beunza, Daniel, and David Stark, "Tools of the Trade: The Socio-Technology of Arbitrage in a Wall Street Trading Room," *Oxford Journals, Industrial and Corporate Change*, 13.2, 2004.

Bick, Jonathan D, "Why Should the Internet Be Any Different?" *Pace Law Review*, 1998-99, HeinOnline.

"Black Monday: The Stock Market Crash of October 19, 1987," U.S. Senate Hearing, Committee on Banking, Housing, and Urban Affairs, Feb., 2-5, 1988, www.web.lexisnexis.com/congcomp/attachment/a.pdf?_m=e28c793ad9e7572f57e6d8a3df5dce81&wc hp=dGLzVlzzSkSA&_md5=f943b95389b86cf5f4134cde610a75f 7&ie=a.pdf.

Bond, Stephen R., and Jason G. Cummins, "The Stock Market and Investment in the New Economy: Some Tangible Facts and Intangible Fictions," *Brookings Papers on Economic Activity*, 2000.1, 2000.

Bookstaber, Richard, *A Demon of Our Own Design: Markets, Hedge Funds, and the Perils of Financial Innovation* (New York: John Wiley and Sons, Inc., 2007).

Brady, Robert A., "Reports and Conclusions of the Temporary National Economic Committee," *The Economic Journal*, 53.212, Dec. 1943.

Bray, Chad, "Ex-NYSE Traders Are Cleared," *Wall Street Journal*, July 31, 2008, www.online.wsj.com/article/SB121745512296898471 .html?mod=MKTW.

Bresiger, Gregory, "Small Is Beautiful: Mini-Primes Eschew Clients with Exotic Strategies," *Traders Magazine*, May 1, 2008.

Brewster, Mike, "Joseph Kennedy's Enduring Example," *Business-Week*, May 29, 2003.

____, "Wall Street's First Cleanup Man," *BusinessWeek*, Mar. 17, 2003.

Brooks, John, *Once in Golconda: a True Drama of Wall Street 1920-1938* (New York: Harper & Row Publishers, 1969).

Bruno, Mark, "Clean-up Hitter: Face to Face with Kevin Parker," *Pensions and Investments*, May 14, 2007, www.pionline.com/apps/pbcs.dll/article?AID=/20070514/FACETOFACE/70511030/1021/TOC.

Bryan, William Jennings, "Cross of Gold Speech," Democratic National Convention, Chicago, July 9, 1896, www.historymatters.gmu.edu/d/5354/.

Calio, Vince, "Pension Fund Execs Find New Strategies Need Prime Brokers," *Pensions and Investment*, Dec. 11, 2006, www.lexisnexis.com/us/lnacademic/results/docview/docview.do?docLinkInd=tru e&risb=21_T4163224372&format=GNBFI&sort=RELEVANCE &startDocNo=1&resultsUrlKey=29_T4163224375&cisb=22_T4 163224374&treeMax=true&treeWidth=0&csi=8094&docNo=7.

Carosso, Vincent, "Washington and Wall Street: The New Deal and Investment Bankers, 1933-1940," *President and Fellows of Harvard College: The Business History Review*, vol. 44, no. 4, Winter 1970.

____, "The Wall Street Money Trust from Pujo through Medina," *The Business History Review* (Boston: Harvard, 1973).

Chernow, Ron, *Alexander Hamilton* (New York: Penguin Group, 2005).

____, *The House of Morgan: An American Banking Dynasty and the Rise of Modern Finance* (New York: Grove Press, 1990).

Chisholm, Andrew M., *Derivatives Demystified: A Step-by-Step Guide to Forwards, Futures, Swaps and Options* (West Sussex: John Wiley and Sons Ltd., 2004).

Clark, Josh, "Why Do Corporations Have the Same Rights as You?" *How Stuff Works*, May 4, 2009, www.money.howstuffworks.com/corporation-person1.htm.

Clark, Nick, "A Legitimate Practice That Could Cause Market Chaos," *The Independent*, June 14, 2008.

Cobb, William, "How the Mortician Helped to Bury Ask," *OCT Review*, 1983, included in House subcommittee hearing on short selling.

Coggan, Philip, "Technically, These Methods Don't Work," *Financial Times*, June 7, 2003, www.proquest.umi.com/pqdweb?index=1&did=344704131&SrchMode=1&sid=2&Fmt=3&VInst=PROD&VType=PQD&RQT=309&VName=PQD&TS=1217533100&clientId=12498.

"Collapse of Enron," Committee on Commerce, Science, and Transportation, Senate, Feb. 12, 2002.

Corbett, Charlie, "Black Monday: 20 Years On," *Investor Weekly*, Oct. 1, 2007, www.investordaily.com.au/cps/rde/xchg/id/style/3129.htm?rdeCOQ=SID-3F579BCE-0CEB03EF.

"The Counterparty's Over; Hedge Funds," *The Economist*, June 14, 2008. www.lexisnexis.com/us/lnacademic/results/docview/docview.do?docLinkInd=true&risb=21_T4261279353&format=GNBFI&sort=RELEVANCE&startDocNo=51&resultsUrlKey=29_T4261279356&cisb=22_T4262276641&treeMax=true&treeWidth=0&csi=7955&docNo=65.

Cox, Adam, "SEC Poised to Review Foreign Broker Rules," *Reuters*, June 19, 2008, www.lexisnexis.com/us/lnacademic/results/docview/docview.do?docLinkInd=true&risb=21_T4269777052&format=

GNBFI&sort=RELEVANCE&startDocNo=1&resultsUrlKey=29
_T4269777055&cisb=22_T4269777054&treeMax=true&treeWi
dth=0&csi=303830&docNo=1.

Crockett, Andrew, "The Evolution and Regulation of Hedge Funds," *Financial Stability Review—Special Issue on Hedge Funds*, no. 10, Apr. 2007, www.banquedefrance.fr/gb/publications/telechar/rsf/2007/etud2_0407.pdf.

Curley, Peter, "The Buyside and the Three Phase-Evolution of Electronic Trading," *The Journal of Trading*, Winter 2007, www.nirvana solutions.com/web/sites/www.nirvanasolutions.com.web/files/JOT_WI_07_Curleyweb2_0.pdf.

D'Avolio, Gene, "The Market for Borrowing Stock," Graduate School of Business, Harvard University, *Journal of Financial Economics* (Boston: Harvard University Graduate School of Business, Nov.-Dec. 2002), 66.2-3, www.sciencedirect.com/science?_ob=Article URL&_udi=B6VBX-473MBMS6&_user=145269&_rdoc=1&_fmt=&_orig=search&_sort=d&view=c&_acct=C000012078&_ve rsion=1&_urlVersion=0&_userid=145269&md5=e9d0a2011ed1b eaf0f81e65eae932101.

"DeAm Plans First Climate Change Private Equity Fund," *Financial Times*, Mar. 27, 2008, www.penews.com/archive/tag/Kevin_Parker/1/content/2350173225.

De Bedts, Ralph F., "The First Chairmen of the Securities and Exchange Commission: Successful Ambassadors of the New Deal to Wall Street," *American Journal of Economics and Sociology*, vol. 23, no. 2, Apr. 1964, 165-78.

Delong, Bradford J., "Financial Crises in the 1890s and the 1990s: Must History Repeat?" *Brookings Papers on Economic Activity*, vol. 1999, no. 2, 1999, 253-79.

de Santis, Vincent, "American Politics in the Gilded Age," *The Review of Politics* (Boston: Cambridge University Press, Oct. 1963), vol. 25, no. 4, 551-61.

Drucker, Jesse, "Offshore Funds Seek Tax Benefit," *Wall Street Journal*, Apr. 16, 2008, www.proquest.umi.com/pqdweb?index=12&did =1462732571&SrchMode=1&sid=3&Fmt=4&VInst=PROD& VType=PQD&RQT=309&VName=PQD&TS=1217607354&cli entId=12498.

Edwards, Franklin R., "Hedge Funds and the Collapse of Long-Term Capital Management," *Journal of Economic Perspectives*, vol. 13, no. 2, Spring, 1999.

"Ex-Knight," *Time*, Mar. 21, 1938.

"Favor Untermyer for Stock Inquiry," *New York Times*, Apr. 14, 1932.

Ferrara, Peter J., and John E. Buttarazzi, "The Senate's New Banking Bill: A Timid Reform," Apr. 27, 1988, Issue Bulletin 140, www.heritage.org/Research/Economy/IB140.cfm?renderforprint=1.

Figlewski, Stephen, "The Informational Effects of Restrictions on Short Sales: Some Empirical Evidence," *The Journal of Financial and Qualitative Analysis*, 16.4, Nov. 1981.

"Find Rockefeller Too Ill to Answer," *New York Times*, Feb. 8, 1913.

Fletcher, Laurence, "Hedge Funds Find New Moneymaking Openings," *The Edge Singapore*, Apr. 14, 2008.

____, "Hedge Investors Hunt for Next Blockbuster Strategy," *The Edge Singapore*, June 23, 2008.

Ford, Lacy K., Jr., "Frontier Democracy: The Turner Thesis Revisited," *Journal of the Early Republic*, 13.2, Summer 1993.

Fox, Justin, "How the 1987 Crash Brought Us Back to the 1800s," *Time*, Oct. 19, 2007, www.time-blog.com/curious_capitalist/ 2007/10/how_the_1987_crash_brought_us.html.

Fraser, Steve, *Wall Street: America's Dream Palace* (New Haven: Yale University Press, 2008).

"Frederick Jackson Turner," *Encyclopedia Britannica*, May 4, 2009, www.britannica.com/EBchecked/topic/610263/Frederick-Jackson-Turner.

Freeman, David F., Jr., "Banking Developments," *The Investment Lawyer*, 12.3, Mar. 2005.

Freund, William C., "Trading Equities: How Soon Will Computerized Trading Become a Reality?" *Institutional Investor*, 25.1, Jan. 1991.

Friese, Shartsis, et al., *U.S. Regulation of Hedge Funds: United States Regulation of Hedge Funds*, American Bar Association, 2005, www.books.google.com/books?id=_Mz09XY9B0AC.

Fund, William, and David A. Hsieh, "The Risk in Hedge Fund Strategies: Theory and Evidence from Long/Short Equity Hedge Funds," Wharton School of Business, www.finance.wharton.upenn.edu/~rlwctr/DHsieh.pdf.

Furbush, Dean, and Annette Poulsen, "Harmonizing Margins: The Regulation of Margin Levels on Stock Index Futures Markets," *Cornell Law Review*, 74.5, July 1989, www.heinonline.org/HOL/Page?collection=journals&handle=hein.journals/clqv74&id=951.

Galbraith, John Kenneth, *The Great Crash: 1929* (New York: Houghton Mifflin Company, 1997).

Gammill, James F., and Terry A. Marsh. "Trading Activity and Price Behavior in the Stock and Stock Index Futures Markets in October 1987," *The Journal of Economic Perspectives*, vol. 2, no. 3, Summer 1988, 25-44, www.jstor.org/sici?sici=08953309(198822)2%3A3%3C25%3ATAAPBI%3E2.0.CO%3B2-N.

Garcia, Beatrice E., "An Appraisal: Analyst May Have Helped Spur Historic Index Drop," *Wall Street Journal*, July 14, 1986, www.proquest.umi.com/pqdweb?index=3&did=27255041&Srch Mode=1&sid=2&Fmt=3&VInst=PROD&VType=PQD&RQT= 309&VName=PQD&TS=1217533100&clientId=12498.

"Gas Man's Trial," *Time*, May 13, 1935, www.time.com/time/ magazine/article/0,9171,754773-2,00.html.

Geisst, Charles R., *Monopolies in America: Empire Builders & Their Enemies from Jay Gould to Bill Gates* (New York: Oxford University Press, 2000).

Getmansky, Mila, "Limits to Arbitrage: Understand How Hedge Funds Fail," Sloan School of Business, www.systemdynamics.org/ conferences/2003/proceed/PAPERS/321.pdf.

Gittleman, Charles S., Julia E. Moran, and Eva Don-Siemion, "SEC Loosens Regulation of Foreign Broker-Dealers," *International Financial Law Review*, Proquest, New York Public Library Science, Industry & Business, 16.10, Oct. 1997, www.proquest.umi. com/pqdweb?index=4&did=23042233&SrchMode=1&sid=1&F mt=3&VInst=PROD&VType=PQD&RQT=309&VName=PQD &TS=1217437894&clientId=12498.

Goetzmann, William N., Roger G. Ibbotson, and Stephen J. Brown, "Offshore Hedge Funds: Survival & Performance 1989-1995 (Undated)," *Yale School of Management Working Paper* no. F-52B.

Goodwin, Doris Kearns, *The Fitzgeralds and the Kennedys: An American Saga* (New York: Simon & Schuster, 1987), 235.

Gordon, John Steele, *The Scarlet Woman of Wall Street: Jay Gould, Jim Fisk, Cornelius Vanderbilt, the Erie Railway Wars, and the Birth of Wall Street* (New York: Weidenfeld and Nicholson, 1988).

Greene, Edward F., "Beyond Borders: Time to Tear Down the Barriers to Global Investing," *Harvard International Law Journal*, 48.1, Winter 2007, www.heinonline.org/HOL/Page?collection=journals& handle=hein.journals/hilj48&div=12&size=2&rot=0&type=image.

Greene, Nathan, Azam H. Aziz, and Gretchen Liersaph, "Hedge Fund Organizational Decisions and How They Affect the Sponsor's Compliance Needs," *Journal of Securities Compliance*, 1.3, May 2008, www.henrystewart.metapress.com/app/home/contribution.asp?referr er=parent&backto=issue,5,9;journal,1,3;linkingpublicationresults, 1:120875,1.

Greenwood, Jeremy, and Boyan Jovanovic, "The Information-Technology Revolution and the Stock Market," *The American Economic Review*, 892, May 1999, www.jstor.org/sici?sici=00028282 (199905)89%3A2%3C116%3ATIRATS%3E2.0.CO%3B2-1.

Haddock, David D, "An Economic Analysis of the Brady Report: Public Interest, Special Interest, or Rent Extraction?" *Cornell Law Review*, vol. 74, no. 5, July 1989, 841, www.heinonline.org/HOL/ Page?collection=journals&handle=hein.journals/clqv74&id=951.

Hamilton, Dane, "Hedge Fund's Fleeing Bear's Prime Broker Business," *The Edge Singapore*, Mar. 24, 2008.

Hansard, Sara, "Federal Oversight of Hedge Funds Still Being Sought; Rejection of Reg Pulls Congress into Debate," *Investment News*, July 10, 2006, www.lexisnexis.com/us/lnacademic/results/docview/ docview.do?docLinkInd=true&risb=21_T4285965863&format= GNBFI&sort=RELEVANCE&startDocNo=1&resultsUrlKey=29 _T4285965872&cisb=22_T4285965871&treeMax=true&treeWi dth=0&csi=224239&docNo=8.

Harman, S. Palmer, "Practice of Short Selling Again Attacked as Unethical," *New York Times*, Oct. 4, 1931.

Harris, Lawrence, "The Dangers of Regulatory Overreaction to the October 1987 Crash," *Cornell Law Review*, 74.5, July 1989, www.heinonline.org/HOL/Page?collection=journals&handle=hei n.journals/clqv74&id=951.

Hartmann, Thom, *Unequal Protection: The Rise of Corporate Dominance and the Theft of Human Rights* (New York: St. Martin's Press, 2002).

"The Heavy Brigade; Hedge-Fund Regulation," *The Economist*, May 26, 2007, www.lexisnexis.com/us/lnacademic/results/docview/ docview.do?docLinkInd=true&risb=21_T4261279353&format= GNBFI&sort=RELEVANCE&startDocNo=176&resultsUrlKey= 29_T4261279356&cisb=22_T4262276641&treeMax=true&tree Width=0&csi=7955&docNo=187.

"Hedge Funds—Risk Roles Change in Crisis Fallout," *The Banker*, May 1, 2008, www.lexisnexis.com/us/lnacademic/results/docview/ docview.do?docLinkInd=true&risb=21_T4261279353&format= GNBFI&sort=RELEVANCE&startDocNo=1&resultsUrlKey=29 _T4261279356&cisb=22_T4261279355&treeMax=true&treeWi dth=0&csi=234197&docNo=4.

Hofstadter, Richard, "The Paranoid Style in American Politics," *Harper's Magazine*, Nov. 1964.

Huerner, Jason, "Tighter Rule May Push Funds Offshore," *Financial Times*, Oct. 1, 2002, www.proquest.umi.com/pqdweb?index=3& did=200028581&SrchMode=1&sid=2&Fmt=3&VInst=PROD& VType=PQD&RQT=309&VName=PQD&TS=1217598826&cli entId=12498.

"IBA, 17 Investment Banking Firms Charged with Monopoly of Underwriting Business; Accused by Government of Conspiracy to Restrain Stock Offerings," *Wall Street Journal*, Oct. 31, 1947, 14.

"In and About Wall Street," *New York Times*, June 23, 1894, www.query .nytimes.com/mem/archivefree/pdf?_r=1&res=9502E1D61630E0 33A25750C2A9609C94659ED7CF&oref=slogin.

"Industry Voice—Prime Time for Hedge Funds," *European Pensions and Investment News*, May 5, 2008, www.lexisnexis.com/us/ lnacademic/results/docview/docview.do?docLinkInd=true&risb=2 1_T4261279353&format=GNBFI&sort=RELEVANCE&start DocNo=26&resultsUrlKey=29_T4261279356&cisb=22_T42622 76641&treeMax=true&treeWidth=0&csi=242802&docNo=43.

"Informal Bargaining Process: An Analysis of the SEC's Regulation of the New York Stock Exchange," *The Yale Law Journal*, 80.4, Mar. 1971.

Jacobs, Bruce I., and Kenneth N. Levy, *Market Neutral Strategies* (New York: John Wiley and Sons, Inc., 2005), www.books.google.com/ books?id=XfYv9e-WuksC.

_____, "Enhanced Active Equity Strategies: Relaxing the Long-Only Constraint in the Pursuit of Active Return," *The Journal of Portfolio Management*, Spring 2006, www.jlem.com/articles/jlem/ EnhancedActive.pdf.

Janeway, Michael, *The Fall of the House of Roosevelt: Brokers of Ideas and Power from FDR to LBJ* (New York: Columbia University Press, 2004).

Jeffries, John W., "The 'New' New Deal: FDR and American Liberalism, 1937-1945," *Political Science Quarterly*, 105.3, Autumn 1990.

Jennings, William W., and William Reichenstein, "The Literature of Private Wealth Management," www.cfapubs.org/doi/pdf/10.2470/ rflr.v1.n3.4362.

Jones, Charles, "The SEC Brings Back the 1930s," Columbia Business School Public Offering, July 18, 2008, www4.gsb.columbia.edu/ publicoffering/post/139305/The+SEC+Brings+Back+the+1930s.

Jones, Charles M., "Shorting Restrictions, Liquidity, and Returns," Graduate School of Business, Columbia University, and NYSE, June 2003, www.wpweb2.tepper.cmu.edu/wfa/wfapdf/shortliq3.pdf.

Jones, Charles M., and Owen A. Lamont, "Short-Sale Constraints and Stock Returns," *Journal of Financial Economics*, 2001.

Josephson, Matthew, "Fifty Years of Wall Street," *The New Yorker*, Oct. 1, 1932, www.newyorker.com/archive/1932/10/01/1932_10_01_022_TNY_CARDS_000218816.

"Kahn at Senate Hearings Urges Law Change to Make Rich Pay More Income Tax," *New York Times*, June 30, 1933.

Kennedy, David, *Freedom From Fear: The American People in Depression and War, 1929-1945* (New York: Oxford University Press, 1999).

Kindleberger, Charles P., *Manias, Panics, and Crashes: A History of Financial Crises* (New York: John Wiley and Sons, Inc., 1978).

Krebs, Albin, "Richard Whitney, 86, Dies; Headed Stock Exchange," *New York Times*, Dec. 6, 1974.

Kupiec, Paul H., and A. Patricia White, "Regulatory Competition and the Efficiency of Alternative Derivative Product Margining Systems," June 11, 1996, www.federalreserve.gov/PUBS/FEDS/1996/199611/199611pap.pdf.

Labate, John, "Hunt for SEC Chief Breaks Tradition," *Financial Times*, Feb. 7, 2001.

"List of Shorts on the Stock Exchange on April 8 as Given Out by the Senate," *New York Times*, Apr. 22, 1932, 12.

Lokey, Eugene M., "Along the Highways of Finance," *New York Times*, Oct. 1, 1931.

____, "Short Selling Again Debated," *New York Times*, Dec. 27, 1931.

_____, "Short Selling Often a Subject for Debate," *New York Times*, July 19, 1931.

Longstreth, Bevis, "A Look at the SEC's Adaptation to Global Market Pressures," *Columbia Journal of Transnational Law*, 1995, 33:319, www.heinonline.org/HOL/Page?collection=journals&handle=hein .journals/cjtl33&div=17&size=2&rot=0&type=image.

Lowenfels, Lewis D, "SEC No-Action Letters: Conflicts with Existing Statutes, Cases, and Commission Releases," *Virginia Law Review*, 59.2, Feb. 1973, www.jstor.org/sici?sici=0042-6601(197302)59% 3A2%3C303%3ASNLCWE%3E2.0.CO%3B2-H.

Lux, Hal, "Confessions of an ex-CIO," *Institutional Investor*, Oct. 1997, www.proquest.umi.com/pqdweb?index=6&did=22387729 &SrchMode=1&sid=4&Fmt=3&VInst=PROD&VType=PQD& RQT=309&VName=PQD&TS=1218119347&clientId=12498.

Macey, Jonathan R., Mark Mitchell, and Jeffry Netter, "Restrictions on Short Sales: An Analysis of the Uptick Rule and Its Role in View of the 1987 Stock Market Crash," *Cornell Law Review*, 74.5, July 1989, www.heinonline.org/HOL/Page?collection=journals& handle=hein.journals/clqv74&id=951.

Mackay, Charles, *Extraordinary Popular Decisions and the Madness of Crowds* (New York: Harmony Books, 1980).

"Margin: Borrowing Money to Pay for Stocks," United States Securities and Exchange Commission, www.sec.gov/investor/pubs/ margin.htm.

"Matters Relating to the October 19 Market Break," Oversight hearings, Committee on Agriculture, Nutrition, and Forestry Senate, Apr. 27, 1988.

McCartney, Robert J., "Nightmare on Wall Street: What If the Tokyo Market Crashes?" *Washington Post*, Jan. 28, 1990.

McCraw, Thomas K., "With Consent of the Governed: SEC's Formative Years," *Journal of Policy Analysis and Management*, 1.3, Spring 1982, www.jstor.org/sici?sici=0276-8739(198221)1%3A3 %3C346%3AWCOTGS%3E2.0.CO%3B2-1.

"*McCulloch* v. *Maryland,*" *Columbia Encyclopedia*, sixth edition, 2008, May 4, 2009, www.encyclopedia.com.

McManus, G., "Is This the Tokyo Stock Market's Last Hurrah?" *Herald Sun*, Sept. 12, 1992.

"Medina Acts to Shorten Anti-Trust Suit Against 17 Investment Bankers; Bars U.S. from Using Evidence Pre-Dating 1935: Moved by Talk of 4-Year Trial," *Wall Street Journal*, Oct. 4, 1951, 5.

"Medina Throws Out Federal Anti-Trust Suit Against 17 Top Investment Banking Firms; Wind-Up of 3-Year Trial Bars Similar Action by U.S. in the Future," *Wall Street Journal*, Sept. 23, 1953, 20.

"Medina's Opinion; Judge Explains Dismissal of U.S. Suit Against Investment Bankers," *Wall Street Journal*, Oct. 15, 1953, 16.

Meeker, James Edward, *The Work of the Stock Exchange* (New York: The Ronald Press Company, 1922), 96.

Merrill, Susan L., and Joseph S. Cohn, "Securities: SEC Opens Door to non-U.S. Brokers," *International Commercial Litigation*, June 1997, issue 20, www.proquest.umi.com/pqdweb?index=5&did= 12974238&SrchMode=1&sid=1&Fmt=3&VInst=PROD&VTyp e=PQD&RQT=309&VName=PQD&TS=1217437894&clientId =12498.

Mildenberg, David, "Bank of America Sells Prime Brokerage to BNP Paribas," *Bloomberg*, June 10, 2008.

"Milestones in Short-Selling History," *Reuters*, July 16, 2008.

Miller, Sam Scott, and Andrew Farber, "Regulation of Foreign Broker-Dealers in the United States," *New York Law School Review*, 34.3,

1989, www.heinonline.org/HOL/Page?collection=journals&handle
=hein.journals/nyls34&div=21&size=2&rot=0&type=image.

Moment, David, "The Business of Whaling in America in the 1850s,"
The Business History Review, vol. 31, no. 3 (Autumn 1957), 261-
91, The President and Fellows of Harvard College.

"Money Monopoly, an Impossibility, Morgan Asserts," *New York
Times*, Dec. 20, 1920.

Morrow, Lance, "The Chronicles of a Dynasty in the Making," *Time*,
Jan. 15, 2001.

Murad, Anatol, "What Keynes Means," *Margin: Borrowing Money to
Pay for Stocks* (New York: Bookman Associates, 1962), United
States Securities and Exchange Commission, www.sec.gov/
investor/pubs/margin.htm.

Neff, Robert, "Japan: Will It Lose Its Competitive Edge?" *Business-
Week*, Apr. 27, 1992.

"New Blood in Wall Street," *New York Times*, Nov. 6, 1904, www.query
.nytimes.com/gst/abstract.html?res=9A07EEDE123BE733A25755C
0A9679D946597D6CF.l

Newman, Anne, "NASD Set to Propose Uptick Rule—Association Asserts
Companies Want It Citing Fear of Shorts," *Wall Street Journal*,
Dec. 31, 1990, www.proquest.umi.com/pqdweb?index=0&did=275
82877&SrchMode=2&sid=6&Fmt=3&VInst=PROD&VType=PQ
D&RQT=309&VName=PQD&TS=1216060358&clientId=12498.

Nicholas, Phil, Jr., "The Agency That Kept Going: The Late New
Deal SEC and Shareholder Democracy," *The Journal of Policy
History*, 16.3, 2004.

Norris, Floyd, "SEC Ends Decades-Old Price Limits on Short Selling," *New York Times*, June 14, 2007, www.nytimes.com/2007/06/
14/business/14sec.html.

"NYT on Short Selling," *New York Times*, Oct. 18, 1930, www.big
picture.typepad.com/comments/2008/09/short-selling-o.html.

"Paint It Black; Buttonwood," *The Economist*, Oct. 20, 2007, 385.8551,
www.proquest.umi.com/pqdweb?index=6&did=1368628731&Src
hMode=1&sid=3&Fmt=3&Vinst=PROD&VType=PQD&RQT
=309&VName=PQD&TS=1217529917&clientId=12498.

Papini, Jessica, "Hedge Funds' Backup Plan: In Troubled Market,
More Funds Look to Diversify Their Prime Brokerage Relationships," *Investment Dealers Digest*, Apr. 14, 2008.

"Parker Associates Fill DeAM's Global Posts," Oct. 11, 2004,
www.news.traderdaily-uk.efinancialcareers.com/ITEM_FR/news
ItemId-3539.

Partnoy, Frank, *Infectious Greed* (New York: Henry Holt and Company, 2003), 209.

Paustian, Chuck, "IRS Ruling Eases Fear," *Pensions & Investment Age*,
Oct. 3, 1988, www.lexisnexis.com/us/lnacademic/results/docview/
docview.do?docLinkInd=true&risb=21_T4162886285&format=
GNBFI&sort=RELEVANCE&startDocNo=1&resultsUrlKey=29
_T4162886219&cisb=22_T4162886218&treeMax=true&treeWi
dth=0&csi=8094&docNo=10.

Pecora, Ferdinand, *Wall Street Under Oath: The Story of Our Modern
Money Changers* (New York: Simon & Schuster, Inc., 1939).

"People to Watch in 2005: Names to Hit the Headlines," Jan. 2, 2005,
www.hermitagefund.com/index.pl/news/article.html?id=559.

Perkins, Edwin J., "Lost Opportunities for Compromise in the Bank
War: A Reassessment of Jackson's Veto Message," *The Business
History Review*, vol. 61, no. 4, Winter 1985, 531-50.

Petzel, Todd E., "Risk Management and Alternative Investments,"
Hedge Fund Management, Apr. 2002, www.cfapubs.org/doi/abs/
10.2469/cp.v2002.n2.3183.

Phelan, John J., Jr., "October 1987, A Retrospective," www.sec
historical.org/collection/papers/2000/2007_0802_Phelan1987.pdf.

"Plan New Tactics in Market Inquiry," *New York Times*, Apr. 25, 1932.

Power, Helen, "JPMorgan Moves to Tie Down Clients," *The Daily
Telegraph*, Mar. 18, 2008.

Power, William, "Uptick Rule Exemption Ticks Off Program-Trade
Foes," *Wall Street Journal*, Nov. 16, 1989, www.proquest.umi.com/
pqdweb?index=0&did=860531002&SrchMode=1&sid=1&Fmt=
10&Vinst=PROD&VType=PQD&RQT=309&VName=HNP&
TS=1216317129&clientId=12498.

"Practice of Short Selling Again Attacked as Unethical," *New York
Times*, Oct. 4, 1931.

Pratt, Tom, *The Investment Dealers' Digest: IDD* (New York), vol. 60,
issue 15, Apr. 11, 1994, 11.

Prechter, Robert, "Hell Hath No Wrath Like an Elliott Wave Theo-
rist Scorned," *Barron's National Business and Financial Weekly*,
Feb. 9, 1987, www.ezproxy.stanford.edu:2162/pqdweb?index=0&
did=409348751&SrchMode=1&sid=1&Fmt=10&VInst=PROD
&VType=PQD&RQT=309&VName=PQD&TS=1217535185&
clientId=12498.

"Prime Brokerage—Electronic Trading—Breaking into the U.S,"
Financial Times, July 1, 2008, www.lexisnexis.com/us/lnacademic/
results/docview/docview.do?docLinkInd=true&risb=21_T426752
1912&format=GNBFI&sort=BOOLEAN&startDocNo=1&result
sUrlKey=29_T4267514370&cisb=22_T4267514369&treeMax=tr
ue&treeWidth=0&csi=242802&docNo=23.

"Prime Numbers—Prime Brokerage Was Virtually Unheard of Until
About a Decade Ago," *The Banker*, Oct. 1, 2004.

"Pujo's Men Besiege Wm. Rockefeller," *New York Times*, Dec. 31,
1912.

Raghavan, Anita, "Hedge Funds Could Lose Offshore Shelter; Senate Panel Weighs Targeting Derivatives By Change in Tax Rules," *Wall Street Journal*, Oct. 1, 2007, www.proquest.umi.com/pqdweb?index=4&did=1348351831&SrchMode=1&sid=2&Fmt=3&Vinst=PROD&VType=PQD&RQT=309&VName=PQD&TS=1217598826&clientId=12498.

Ramirez, Carlos D., "Did J.P. Morgan's Men Add Liquidity? Corporate Investment, Cash Flow, and Financial Structure at the Turn of the Twentieth Century," *The Journal of Finance*, June 1995, www.jstor.org/stable/2329423?origin=JSTOR-below-page.

Ramsay, John, "Rule 15a-6 and the International Marketplace: Time for a New Idea?" *Law and Policy in International Business*, 33.3, Spring 2002, www.proquest.umi.com/pqdweb?index=2&did=265951381&SrchMode=1&sid=1&Fmt=3&VInst=PROD&VType=PQD&RQT=309&VName=PQD&TS=1217437894&clientId=12498.

"Records of the Temporary National Economic Committee," *The National Archives*, Record Group 144, 1938-41, www.archives.gov/research/guide-fed-records/groups/144.html#144.2.

Renshaw, Patrick, "Was There a Keynesian Economy in the USA between 1933 and 1945?" *Journal of Contemporary History*, 34.3, July 1999.

Report of the Pujo Committee, 1913, 1997, vol. 1, issue 1, 38, www.search.ebscohost.com/login.aspx?direct=true&db=aph&jid=26LZ&site=ehost-live.

Rev. Rul. 95-8, 1995-1 C.B. 107 www.irs.gov/pub/irs-tege/rr95-08.pdf.

Ritchie, Donald A., "Reforming the Regulatory Process: Why James Landis Changes His Mind," *The Business History Review*, 54.3, Autumn 1980.

The Roaring Twenties Began with a Commodities Bust, ed. Justice Litle, Nov. 5, 2008, Taipain Publishing Group, Apr. 30, 2009, www.taipanpublishinggroup.com/Taipan-Daily-110508.html.

Rock, Edward B., "Encountering the Scarlet Woman of Wall Street: Speculative Comments at the End of the Century," *Theoretical Inquiries in Law*, 2.1, Jan. 2001.

Rockoff, Hugh, "The 'Wizard of Oz' as a Monetary Allegory," *The Journal of Political Economy*, vol. 98, no. 4, Aug. 1990, 739-60.

Rohrer, Julie, "They're Back! The Offshore-Fund Bonanza," *Institutional Investor*, Jan. 1992, 26.1, www.proquest.umi.com/pqdweb? index=0&did=526597&SrchMode=1&sid=2&Fmt=3&VInst=PR OD&VType=PQD&RQT=309&VName=PQD&TS=12175988 26&clientId=12498.

Romano, Roberta, "The Politics of the Brady Report: A Comment," *Cornell Law Review*, Symposium on the Regulation of Secondary Trading Markets: Program Trading, Volatility, Portfolio Insurance, And the Role of Specialists and Market Makers, vol. 74, no. 5, July 1989, 865, www.heinonline.org/HOL/Page?collection=journals &handle=hein.journals/clqv74&id=951.

Roosevelt, Franklin Delano, "Only Thing We Have to Fear Is Fear Itself," First Inaugural Address, 1933, www.historymatters.gmu .edu/d/5057/.

Rotbart, Dean, "Market Hardball: Aggressive Methods of Some Short Sellers Stir Critics to Cry Foul: Loosely Allied Traders Pick a Stock, Then Show Doubt in an Effort to Depress It: Gray Areas of Securities Law," *Wall Street Journal*, Sept. 5, 1985.

Royster, Vermont, "Same Song, Second Verse: After the Crash?" *Wall Street Journal*, Nov. 25, 1987, www.proquest.umi.com/pqdweb? index=7&did=27321237&SrchMode=2&sid=3&Fmt=3&VInst=

PROD&VType=PQD&RQT=309&VName=PQD&TS=121579
8253&clientId=12498.

Santoli, Michael, "Getting a Handle on 1987," *Barron's*, Oct. 1, 2007,
87.40. www.proquest.umi.com/pqdweb?index=5&did=1367177
111&SrchMode=1&sid=1&Fmt=3&Vinst=PROD&Vype=PQ
D&RQT=309&VName=PQD&TS=1217528465&clientId=
12498.

Sarton, George, *The Whaling Museums of New Bedford and Nantucket* (University of Chicago Press on behalf of the History of Science Society), *Isis*, vol. 16, no. 1, July 1931, 115-23.

"Say Money Trust Is Not Disclosed," *New York Times*, Dec. 1, 1913.

Scannell, Kara, and Jenny Strasburg, "SEC Moves to Curb Short-Selling," *Wall Street Journal*, July 16, 2008.

Schafer, Lee, "Short on Patience: Jim Watkins of Golden Valley Microwave Foods Has Long Been Obsessed with Quashing Short-Sellers of His Company's Stock. He's Getting Closer," *Corporate Report Minnesota*, Nov. 1989.

Schwarz, Ted, *Joseph P. Kennedy: The Mogul, the Mob, the Statesman, and the Making of an American Myth* (New York: John Wiley and Sons, Inc., 2003).

Selgin, George A., and Lawrence H. White, "Laissez-Faire Monetary Theorists in Late Nineteenth-Century America," *Southern Economic Journal*, vol. 56, no. 3, Jan. 1990, 774-87.

Sender, Henny, "The Pragmatic Collosus," *Institutional Investor*, 25.13, Nov. 1991.

_____, "Too Japanese to Fail?" *Institutional Investor*, 25.5, May 1991.

Shiller, Robert J., *Irrational Exuberance* (Princeton, NJ: Princeton University Press, 2005).

"Short Selling Activity in the Stock Market: The Effects on Small Companies and the Need for Regulation," Congressional Information Service, Inc., Committee on Government Operations, House of Representatives, Nov. 28, 29, Dec. 6, 1989, www.web.lexis nexis.com/congcomp/attachment/a.pdf?_m=bce01a70a0d1e5721 c418b2923f78f30&wchp=dGLbVlWzSkSA&_md5=58d8c67681 4ddb46836a48622b9e70dc&ie=a.pdf.

Siegel, Jeremy J., "Equity Risk Premia, Corporate Profit Forecasts, and Investor Sentiment Around the Stock Crash of October 1987," *The Journal of Business*, vol. 65, no. 4, Oct. 1992, 557-70, www.jstor .org/sici?sici=00219398(199210)65%3A4%3C557%3AERPCPF% 3E2.0.CO%3B2-5.

Simpson, Glenn R. and Gregory L. White, "Bermuda May Require Hedge Fund Licenses," *Wall Street Journal*, Nov. 18, 2004, www.proquest.umi.com/pqdweb?index=9&did=737916891&Srch Mode=1&sid=8&Fmt=3&VInst=PROD&VType=PQD&RQT= 309&VName=PQD&TS=1217603087&clientId=12498.

Smith, Amanda, *Hostage to Fortune: The Letters of Joseph P. Kennedy* (New York: Viking, 2001).

Soble, Jonathan, "Nikkei Still Fighting to Recover," *Financial Times*, Oct. 19, 2007.

Sornette, Didier, *Why Stock Markets Crash: Critical Events in Complex Financial Systems* (Princeton, NJ: Princeton University Press, 2003).

Staley, Kathryn F., *The Art of Short Selling* (New York: John Wiley and Sons, Inc., 1996), www.books.google.com/books?id=tOtPb3LQ DC0C&pg=PA249&lpg=PA249&dq=pollack+report&source=web &ots=ckc-B820Gx&sig=BlCJpMk7W8H-WOSSCYztG-epCKg& hl=en&sa=X&oi=book_result&resnum=5&ct=result#PPA249,M1.

Steiner, Michael, "From Frontier to Region: Frederick Jackson Turner and the New Western History," *The Pacific Historical Review*, 64.4, Nov. 1995.

Stewart, James B., and Daniel Hertzberg, "Terrible Tuesday: How the Stock Market Almost Disintegrated a Day After the Crash — Credit Dried Up for Brokers and Especially Specialists Until Fed Came to Rescue — Most Perilous Day in 50 Years," *Wall Street Journal*, Nov. 20, 1987.

"Stock Exchange Itself to Establish Rates to Be Paid for Borrowing of Securities," *New York Times*, June 28, 1931.

"Stock Gambling Not Under Ban," *New York Times*, Dec. 14, 1912, www.query.nytimes.com/gst/abstract.html?res=9407E4DB103CE 633A25757C1A9649D946396D6CF.

Stout, Lynn A., "The Unimportance of Being Efficient: An Economic Analysis of Stock Market Pricing and Securities Regulation," *Michigan Law Review*, vol. 87, no. 3, Dec. 1988, 613-709, www.jstor .org/sici?sici=00262234(198812)87%3A3%3C613%3ATUOBEA %3E2.0.CO%3B2-P.

"Strategies, Allocation, and Performance: Prime Brokerage-Hedge Funds Concern Over Utilization of Their Assets," *Financial Times Mandate*, Mar. 1, 2008.

Strauss, Lawrence C., "Confessions of a Short Seller," *Barron's*, 88.20, May 19, 2008, www.proquest.umi.com/pqdweb?index=2&did= 1482363711&SrchMode=1&sid=2&Fmt=3&Vinst=PROD&V Type=PQD&RQT=309&VName=PQD&TS=1216058184&clie ntId=12498.

"Tax-Exempt Entities, Notional Principal Contracts, and the Unrelated Business Tax Income," *Harvard Law Review*, 105.6, Apr. 1992, www.jstor.org.

Taylor, Carolyn E., "Hedge Fund Managers: Summary and Implications of New Rule Requiring SEC Registration," *The Journal of Investment Compliance*, 5.4, Spring 2005. www.proquest.umi .com/pqdweb?index=15&did=821901141&SrchMode=1&sid=8

&Fmt=2&Vinst=PROD&VType=PQD&RQT=309&VName=P
QD&TS=1217603087&clientId=12498.

Testimony of J. P. Morgan on the Money Trust Investigation to the Subcommittee of the Committee on Banking and Currency, U.S. House of Representatives, courtesy of Securities and Exchange Commission Historical Society, wwww.sechistorical.org.

Thomas, Landon, Jr. "The Man Who Won as Others Lost," *New York Times*, Oct. 13, 2007, www.nytimes.com/2007/10/13/business/ 13speculate.html?pagewanted=1&8br.

"Triumph in Gas," *Time*, Feb. 10, 1936, www.time.com/time/magazine/ article/0,9171,755829-2,00.html.

Tufano, Peter, "Business Failure, Judicial Intervention, and Financial Innovation: Restructuring U.S. Railroads in the Nineteenth Century," *The Business History Review*, 71.1, Spring 1997, www.jstor.org.

Turner, Frederick Jackson, *The Frontier in American History*, www. books.google.com/books?hl=en&lr=&id=gp4Xl30eR0C&oi=fnd&p g=PA1&dq=frederick+jackson+turner,+frontier+thesis&otsZJnXv5 1gJ-&sig=ZGz-mAhrbM-OKDBWlpNdY06zG5o#PPP9,M1.

_____, *The Frontier in American History* (New York: Henry Holt and Company, 1935), www.xroads.virginia.edu/~HYPER/TURNER/ home.html.

Twibell, David A., "Hedge Your Bets: In Today's Market, a Bit of Short Selling in Your Clients' Portfolios May Pay Off," *Financial Planning*, June 1, 2008.

"Twilight of TNEC," *Time*, Apr. 14, 1941.

U.S. Congress, House of Representatives. 101st Congress, First Session, Hearings Before the Commerce, Consumer, and Monetary Affairs Subcommittee (introduced in the U.S. Senate; Nov. 28, 1989), viewed Apr. 2009 *LexisNexis*, New York Public Library Science, Industry, and Business.

"Untermyer Hits Bankers Groups," *New York Times*, Apr. 24, 1932.

"U.S. Anti-Trust Trial Is Opened Against 17 Investment Bankers, IBA Long, Contentious Case Is Indicated," *Wall Street Journal*, Nov. 29, 1950, 9.

"U.S. Says Investment Firms Tried to Bar Competitive Bidders," *Wall Street Journal*, Dec. 2, 1950, 2.

"Vote Wide Inquiry on Short Selling," *New York Times*, Mar. 5, 1932.

Waggoner, John, "Let's Review What We Learned from '87 Crash; Biggest Lesson of All: Marking Timing Not a Good Choice," *USA Today*, Oct. 19, 2007, www.lexisnexis.com/us/lnacademic/results/docview/docview.do?docLinkInd=true&risb=21_T4279208434&format=GNBFI&sort=RELEVANCE&startDocNo=51&resultsUrlKey=29_T4279208438&cisb=22_T4279208437&treeMax=true&treeWidth=0&csi=8213&docNo=70.

"Wall Street Inquiry by Senate Monday: Whitney Summoned," *New York Times*, Apr. 9, 1932.

"Wall St. Discusses Short Stock Sales," *New York Times*, Oct. 4, 1931.

Ward, James A., "Image and Reality: The Railway Corporate-State Metaphor," *The Business History Review*, 55.4, Winter 1981.

Weber, Axel A., "Hedge Funds: A Central Bank Perspective," *Financial Stability Review—Special Issue on Hedge Funds*, no. 10, Apr. 2007, www.banquefrance.fr/gb/publications/telnomot/rsf/2007/rsf_0407.pdf#page=161.

Westbrook, Jesse and David Scheer, "SEC to Limit Short Sales of Fannie, Freddie, Brokers," *Bloomberg*, July 15, 2008, www.bloomberg.com/apps/news?pid=20601087&sid=aPokh6La9.HY&refer=home.

White, James A., "Short-Selling Is Now for the Stodgy—Pension Funds Join Others Using Tactic," *Wall Street Journal*, Apr. 27, 1989, 1, www.proquest.umi.com/pqdweb?index=0&did=27480390&SrchM

ode=2&sid=5&Fmt=3&VInst=PROD&VType=PQD&RQT=309
&VName=PQD&TS=1215798430&clientId=12498.

"Whitney Declares Short Sales Vital," *New York Times*, Oct. 17, 1931.

"Whitney Denounces Legislation Aimed at Short Selling," *New York Times*, Feb. 25, 1932.

"Whitney Testifies 2-Week Drop Cost Market 6 Billions," *New York Times*, Apr. 13, 1932.

Why Today's Crisis Is More Like 1919 Than 1930, ed. Justice Litle, 2007-08, Straightstocks.com, Apr. 14, 2009, www.straightstocks.com/market-commentary/why-today%E2%80%99s-crisis-is-more-like-1919-than-1929/.

Williams, William Appleman, "The Frontier Thesis and American Foreign Policy," *The Pacific Historical Review*, 24.4, Nov. 1955.

Williamson, Christine, "Financing Becomes New Worry for Execs," *Pensions and Investments*, Mar. 31, 2008, www.lexisnexis.com/us/ln academic/results/docview/docview.do?docLinkInd=true&risb=21_T 4261279353&format=GNBFI&sort=RELEVANCE&startDocNo= 26&resultsUrlKey=29_T4261279356&cisb=22_T4262276641&tree Max=true&treeWidth=0&csi=8094&docNo=39.

Wrighton, Jo, "Money Management—Trading Up?" *Institutional Investor*, Nov. 12, 2007, www.iimagazine.com/article.aspx?article ID=1696107.

"You Can't Say 'Crash' in Japanese," *Institutional Investor*, May 1988, 22.5.

Ziemba, William T., and Sandra L. Schwartz. "The Growth in the Japanese Stock Market, 1949-90, and Prospects for the Future," *Managerial and Decision Economics*, 12.2, Apr. 1991.

Zitzewitz, Eric. "Who Cars About Shareholders? Arbitrage-Proofing Mutual Funds," *The Journal of Law, Economics, and Organization* (Oxford University Press, 2003), www.jleo.oxfordjournals.org/cgi/reprint/19/2/245.

Zuckerman, Gregory, "Blame Game: The 'Uptick' Rule Debate," *Wall Street Journal*, Apr. 1, 2008, www.proquest.umi.com/pqdweb ?index=5&did=1454789041&SrchMode=1&sid=4&Fmt=4&Vin st=PROD&VType=PQD&RQT=309&VName=PQD&TS=121 6059298&clientId=12498.

INDEX

ABOUT THE AUTHOR

Robert Sloan is the managing partner of S3 Partners, LLC, a New York and London-based balance sheet manager for top hedge funds globally, which he founded in 2003. In addition, Bob serves as a member of the board for MF Global Ltd., the world's largest exchange-traded derivatives broker. Prior to S3 Partners, Bob was a managing director, the global head of prime brokerage, equity finance and delta one products, and a member of both the securities division operating committee and the product managers committee at Credit Suisse First Boston. In 1998, Bob founded and chaired the CSFB/Tremont Hedge Fund Index. This was the first investable benchmark index for alternative investments. From 1989 until 1996, he worked at Lehman Brothers in the equity derivatives and central funding unit. Prior to his career on Wall Street, Bob was a speech writer and translator for the Ministry of International Trade and Industry (MITI), Tokyo, Japan. Bob holds a Bachelor of Arts degree from Washington & Lee University.